English-Language Development Standards for California Public Schools

Kindergarten Through Grade Twelve

Publishing Information

When the *English-Language Development Standards for California Public Schools, Kindergarten Through Grade Twelve* was adopted by the California State Board of Education in July 1999, the members of the State Board were the following: Robert L. Trigg, President; Kathryn Dronenburg, Vice-President; Marian Bergeson; Susan Hammer; Carlton J. Jenkins; Marion Joseph; Yvonne Larsen; Monica Lozano; Janet Nicholas; Vicki Reynolds; and Richard Weston.

This publication was edited by Faye Ong, working in cooperation with Lilia G. Sanchez, Consultant, Language Policy and Leadership Office. It was designed and prepared for printing by the staff of CDE Press, with the cover and interior design created and prepared by Juan D. Sanchez. Typesetting was done by Jeannette Huff. It was published by the California Department of Education, 1430 N Street, Sacramento, CA 95814-5901. It was distributed under the provisions of the Library Distribution Act and *Government Code* Section 11096.

ISBN 0-8011-1578-7

Ordering Information

Copies of this publication are available for $12.50 each, plus shipping and handling charges. California residents are charged sales tax. Orders may be sent to the California Department of Education, CDE Press, Sales Office, 1430 N Street, Suite 3207, Sacramento, CA 95814-5901; FAX (916) 323-0823. See page 90 for complete information on payment, including credit card purchases, and an order blank. Prices on all publications are subject to change.

A partial list of other educational resources available from the Department appears on page 89. In addition, an illustrated *Educational Resources Catalog* describing publications, videos, and other instructional media available from the Department can be obtained without charge by writing to the address given above or by calling the Sales Office at (916) 445-1260.

Notice

The guidance in *English-Language Development Standards for California Public Schools, Kindergarten Through Grade Twelve* is not binding on local educational agencies or other entities. Except for the statutes, regulations, and court decisions that are referenced herein, the document is exemplary, and compliance with it is not mandatory. (See *Education Code* Section 33308.5.)

Prepared for publication
by CSEA members.

Contents

California English-Language Proficiency Assessment Project

Assembly Bill 748, enacted in 1997, requires that the test or tests assessing the progress of English learners toward achieving fluency in English be aligned with state standards for English-language development. The San Diego County Office of Education, under contract with the Standards and Assessment Division of the California Department of Education, named an advisory committee of state and national leaders to assist in the development of the English-language development (ELD) standards. A list of the California English-Language Proficiency Assessment Project advisory committee members and their affiliations follows:

Adel Nadeau, Chair, San Diego County Office of Education

Tim Allen, San Diego City Unified School District

Bob Anderson, California Department of Education

Nancy Brynelson, California Department of Education

Frances Butler, Center for the Study of Evaluation, University of California, Los Angeles

Ruben Carriedo, San Diego City Unified School District

Richard Diaz, California Department of Education

Richard Duran, University of California, Santa Barbara

Mark Fetler, California Department of Education

Sara Fields, California Association of Teachers of English to Speakers of Other Languages

Jim Grissom, California Department of Education

Elizabeth Hartung-Cole, Long Beach Unified School District

Donna Heath, San Dieguito Union High School District

Natalie Kuhlman, Teaching English to Speakers of Other Languages Board

Magaly Lavadenz, Loyola Marymount University

Barbara Merino, University of California, Davis

Basha Millhollen, California Department of Education

Ofelia Miramontes, University of Colorado, Boulder

Alberto Ochoa, San Diego State University

David Ramirez, California State University, Long Beach

Rosalia Salinas, San Diego County Office of Education

Robin Scarcella, University of California, Irvine

Jerome Shaw, WestEd

Leonore Spafford, Secretary, San Diego County Office of Education

Shelly Spiegel-Coleman, Los Angeles County Office of Education

Gwen Stephens, California Department of Education

Aida Walqui, Stanford University

Terry Wiley, California State University, Long Beach

Sandy Williams, Escondido Union High School District

Richard Wolfe, Ontario Institute for Studies in Education

Gay Wong, California State University, Los Angeles

Charlene Zawacki, Escondido Union School District

Note: The affiliations of persons named in this list were current at the time this document was developed.

Executive Summary

The following pages present a summary of the English-language development (ELD) standards for each domain (listening and speaking, reading, and writing). The summary is designed to give an overview of what students must know and be able to do as they move toward full fluency in English. The levels through which English learners progress are identified as *beginning, intermediate,* and *advanced.* For each ELD standard the summary indicates the English–language arts substrand associated with it.

LISTENING AND SPEAKING

Strategies and Applications

English–language arts substrand	Beginning ELD level*
Comprehension	Answer simple questions with one- to two-word responses.
	Respond to simple directions and questions by using physical actions and other means of nonverbal communication (e.g., matching objects, pointing to an answer, drawing pictures).
	Begin to speak with a few words or sentences by using a few standard English grammatical forms and sounds (e.g., single words or phrases).
	Use common social greetings and simple repetitive phrases independently (e.g., "Thank you," "You're welcome").
	Ask and answer questions by using phrases or simple sentences.
	Retell stories by using appropriate gestures, expressions, and illustrative objects.
Organization and Delivery of Oral Communication	Begin to be understood when speaking, but usage of standard English grammatical forms and sounds (e.g., plurals, simple past tense, pronouns [he or she]) may be inconsistent.
	Orally communicate basic personal needs and desires (e.g., "May I go to the bathroom?").

English–language arts substrand	Intermediate ELD level*
Comprehension	Ask and answer instructional questions by using simple sentences.
	Listen attentively to stories and information and identify important details and concepts by using both verbal and nonverbal responses.
	Ask and answer instructional questions with some supporting elements (e.g., "Which part of the story was the most important?").
Comprehension and Organization and Delivery of Oral Communication	Participate in social conversations with peers and adults on familiar topics by asking and answering questions and soliciting information.
Organization and Delivery of Oral Communication	Make oneself understood when speaking by using consistent standard English grammatical forms and sounds; however, some rules are not followed (e.g., third-person singular, male and female pronouns).

*The ELD standards must be applied appropriately for students in each grade level from kindergarten through grade twelve.

LISTENING AND SPEAKING

Strategies and Applications *(Continued)*

English–language arts substrand	Advanced ELD level*
Comprehension	Demonstrate understanding of most idiomatic expressions (e.g., "Give me a hand") by responding to such expressions and using them appropriately.
Organization and Delivery of Oral Communication	Negotiate and initiate social conversations by questioning, restating, soliciting information, and paraphrasing the communication of others.

*The ELD standards must be applied appropriately for students in each grade level from kindergarten through grade twelve.

Word Analysis, Fluency, and Systematic Vocabulary Development

English–language arts substrand	Beginning ELD level*
Phonemic Awareness and Decoding and Word Recognition	Recognize and produce the English phonemes that are like the phonemes students hear and produce in their primary language. Recognize and produce English phonemes that are unlike the phonemes students hear and produce in their primary language.
Phonemic Awareness, Decoding and Word Recognition, Concepts About Print	Produce most English phonemes while beginning to read aloud.
Vocabulary and Concept Development	Produce simple vocabulary (e.g., single words or very short phrases) to communicate basic needs in social and academic settings (e.g., locations, greetings, classroom objects). Demonstrate comprehension of simple vocabulary with an appropriate action. Retell stories by using simple words, phrases, and sentences. Recognize simple affixes (e.g., *educate, education*), prefixes (e.g., <u>*dis*</u>*like,* <u>*pre*</u>*heat*), synonyms (e.g., *big, large*), and antonyms (e.g., *hot, cold*). Begin to use knowledge of simple affixes, prefixes, synonyms, and antonyms to interpret the meaning of unknown words. Recognize the difference between the use of the first- and third-person points of view in phrases or simple sentences.

*The ELD standards must be applied appropriately for students in each grade level from kindergarten through grade twelve.

Word Analysis, Fluency, and Systematic Vocabulary Development *(Continued)*

English–language arts substrand	Intermediate ELD level*
Phonemic Awareness, Decoding and Word Recognition, Concepts About Print	Produce English phonemes while reading aloud. Recognize sound/symbol relationships and basic word-formation rules in written text (e.g., basic syllabication rules and phonics). Apply knowledge of English phonemes in oral and silent reading to derive meaning from literature and texts in content areas.
Vocabulary and Concept Development	Use more complex vocabulary and sentences to communicate needs and express ideas in a wider variety of social and academic settings. Recognize simple antonyms and synonyms (e.g., *good, bad, blend, mix*) in written text. Expand recognition of them and begin to use appropriately. Apply knowledge of vocabulary to discussions related to reading tasks. Read simple vocabulary, phrases, and sentences independently. Read narrative and expository texts aloud with the correct pacing, intonation, and expression. Use expanded vocabulary and descriptive words in oral and written responses to written texts. Recognize and understand simple idioms, analogies, and figures of speech in written text. Recognize that some words have multiple meanings and apply this knowledge to written text. Recognize the function of connectors in written text (e.g., *first, then, after that, finally*).

*The ELD standards must be applied appropriately for students in each grade level from kindergarten through grade twelve.

Word Analysis, Fluency, and Systematic Vocabulary Development *(Continued)*

English–language arts substrand	Advanced ELD level*
Phonemic Awareness, Decoding and Word Recognition, Concepts About Print	Apply knowledge of sound/symbol relationships and basic word-formation rules to derive meaning from written text (e.g., basic syllabication rules, regular and irregular plurals, and basic phonics).
Vocabulary and Concept Development	Apply knowledge of academic and social vocabulary while reading independently.
	Be able to use a standard dictionary to find the meanings of unfamiliar words.
	Interpret the meaning of unknown words by using knowledge gained from previously read text.
	Understand idioms, analogies, and metaphors in conversation and written text.

*The ELD standards must be applied appropriately for students in each grade level from kindergarten through grade twelve.

Summary
READING

Reading Comprehension

English–language arts substrand	Beginning ELD level*
Comprehension and Analysis of Grade-Level Appropriate Text	Respond orally to stories read aloud and use physical actions and other means of nonverbal communication (e.g., matching objects, pointing to an answer, drawing pictures).
	Respond orally to stories read aloud, giving one- to two-word responses in answer to factual comprehension questions (*who, what, when, where,* and *how*).
	Understand and follow simple one-step directions for classroom-related activities.
Structural Features of Informational Materials	Identify the basic sequence of events in stories read aloud, using important words or visual representations, such as pictures and story frames.
	Respond orally to stories read aloud, using phrases or simple sentences to answer factual comprehension questions.

English–language arts substrand	Intermediate ELD level*
Comprehension and Analysis of Grade-Level-Appropriate Text	Understand and follow simple written directions for classroom-related activities.
	Read text and orally identify the main ideas and draw inferences about the text by using detailed sentences.
	Read and identify basic text features, such as the title, table of contents, and chapter headings.
	Respond to comprehension questions about text by using detailed sentences (e.g., "The brown bear lives with his family in the forest").
Structural Features of Informational Materials	Identify, using key words or phrases, the basic sequence of events in stories read.

*The ELD standards must be applied appropriately for students in each grade level from kindergarten through grade twelve.

Reading Comprehension *(Continued)*

English–language arts substrand	Advanced ELD level*
Comprehension and Analysis of Grade-Level-Appropriate Text	Read and orally respond to familiar stories and other texts by answering factual comprehension questions about cause-and-effect relationships.
	Read and orally respond to stories and texts from content areas by restating facts and details to clarify ideas.
	Explain how understanding of text is affected by patterns of organization, repetition of main ideas, syntax, and word choice.
	Write a brief summary (two or three paragraphs) of a story.

*The ELD standards must be applied appropriately for students in each grade level from kindergarten through grade twelve.

Summary
WRITING

Strategies and Applications

English–language arts substrand	Beginning ELD level*
Penmanship	Copy the alphabet legibly. Copy words posted and commonly used in the classroom (e.g., labels, number names, days of the week).
Organization and Focus	Write simple sentences by using key words commonly used in the classroom (e.g., labels, number names, days of the week, and months). Write phrases and simple sentences that follow English syntactical order.

English–language arts substrand	Intermediate ELD level*
Organization and Focus	Follow a model given by the teacher to independently write a short paragraph of at least four sentences.
Organization and Focus, Penmanship	Write legible, simple sentences that respond to topics in language arts and other content areas (e.g., math, science, history–social science).
Organization and Focus	Create cohesive paragraphs that develop a central idea and consistently use standard English grammatical forms even though some rules may not be followed. Write simple sentences about an event or a character from a written text. Produce independent writing that is understood when read but may include inconsistent use of standard grammatical forms.

English–language arts substrand	Advanced ELD level*
Organization and Focus	Develop a clear thesis and support it by using analogies, quotations, and facts appropriately. Write a multiparagraph essay with consistent use of standard grammatical forms.

*The ELD standards must be applied appropriately for students in each grade level from kindergarten through grade twelve.

WRITING

English-Language Conventions

English–language arts substrand	Beginning, intermediate, and advanced ELD levels*
Capitalization	Use capitalization when writing one's own name.
	Use capitalization at the beginning of a sentence and for proper nouns.
Punctuation	Use a period at the end of a sentence and a question mark at the end of a question.
Capitalization, Punctuation, and Spelling	Produce independent writing that includes partial consistency in the use of capitalization and periods and correct spelling.
	Produce independent writing with consistent use of capitalization, punctuation, and correct spelling.

*The ELD standards must be applied appropriately for students in each grade level from kindergarten through grade twelve.

Introduction

The *English–Language Arts Content Standards for California Public Schools* (1998) and the *Reading/Language Arts Framework for California Public Schools* (1999), both adopted by the State Board of Education, define what all students in California, including students learning English as a second language, are expected to know and be able to do. The English-language development (ELD) standards are designed to supplement the English–language arts content standards to ensure that limited-English proficient (LEP) students (now called English learners in California) develop proficiency in both the English language and the concepts and skills contained in the English–language arts content standards.

The ELD standards were developed by a committee composed of 15 practitioners of and experts in English-language development and assessment. The standards are designed to assist teachers in moving English learners to fluency in English and proficiency in the English–language arts content standards. The ELD standards will also be used to develop the California English-Language Development Examinations. The standards were reviewed by teachers throughout California and were presented to the California State Board of Education in January 1999. After the State Board meeting in January, the draft standards were posted on the Internet for public comment. The standards were approved by the State Board during April 1999 contingent on some modifications and additions to better align the ELD standards with the English–language arts content standards that had been adopted by the State Board in January 1997. The State Board gave final approval to the ELD standards in July 1999.

The *Reading/Language Arts Framework* is based on the assumption that all students will attain proficiency in the English–language arts standards, but the framework also recognizes that not all learners will acquire skills and knowledge at the same rate. There are 1.4 million English learners in California. More than 40 percent of students in California speak a language other than English, and about 25 percent of students in California are not yet fluent in English. Those students enter school with language abilities very different from monolingual English-speaking students, who begin school with speaking vocabularies of between 2,000 and 8,000 words.

Generally, monolingual English speakers have mastered basic English sentence structures before entering school. English learners enter California public schools at all grade levels with limited or no knowledge of English vocabulary and sentence structure. Many of these children are unfamiliar with the Roman alphabet, and those who know the alphabet often have to learn new sounds for many of the letters. English learners need to catch up with the state's monolingual English speakers. The ELD standards address the skills English learners must acquire in initial English learning to enable them to become proficient in the English–language arts standards.

The *Reading/Language Arts Framework* specifies that teachers must provide students with straightforward assessments of their proficiency in English at every stage of instruction so that students understand what to do to improve. The processes by which students develop proficiency in a second language differ from the experiences of monolingual English speakers. Grammatical structures that monolingual English speakers learn early in their language development may be learned much later by students learning English as a second language. Progress to full competency for English learners depends on the age at which a child begins learning English and the richness of the child's English environment. The English-language development standards provide teachers with usable information to ensure that English-language development is occurring appropriately for all students, including English learners who enter school in:

- Kindergarten through grade two
- Grades three through twelve, literate in their primary language
- Grades three through twelve, not literate in their primary language

The ELD standards for grades three through twelve are designed for students who are literate in their primary language. Students who enter California schools in those grade levels not literate in their primary language need to be taught the ELD literacy standards for earlier grade levels, including those standards related to phonemic awareness, concepts of print, and decoding skills.

The *Reading/Language Arts Framework* addresses universal access to mastering the language arts standards. At each grade level suggestions are made to teachers for ensuring that the needs of English learners are addressed. The ELD standards encapsulate those suggestions by explicitly stating what all students need to know and be able to do as they learn English and move toward mastery of the English–language arts standards for their grade levels.

The ELD standards define the levels of proficiency required for an English learner to move through the levels of English-language development. The standards are designed to move all students, regardless of their instructional program, into the mainstream English–language arts curriculum. The levels of proficiency in a second language have been well documented through research, and the ELD standards were designed around those levels to provide teachers in *all* types of programs with clear benchmarks of progress. The ELD standards provide different academic pathways, which reflect critical developmental differences, for students who enter school at various grade levels.

The ELD standards are written as pathways to, or benchmarks of, the English–language arts standards. At the early proficiency levels, one ELD standard may be a pathway to attain several English–language arts standards. At the more advanced levels, the skills in the ELD standards begin to resemble those in the English–language arts standards and represent the standards at which an English learner has attained academic proficiency in English. *The ELD standards integrate listening, speaking, reading, and writing and create a distinct pathway to reading in English rather than delaying the introduction of English reading.*

All English learners, regardless of grade level or primary-language literacy level, must receive reading instruction in English.

English learners are to learn to read in English while they are acquiring oral English fluency. English learners in kindergarten through grade two are to demonstrate proficiency in the English–language arts standards of phonemic awareness, decoding, and concepts of print appropriate for their grade levels. These standards are embedded in the ELD standards. English learners in grades three through twelve must demonstrate proficiency in those essential beginning reading skills by the time they reach the early intermediate level of the ELD standards. This expectation holds true for students who enter school regardless of whether they are literate or not literate in their primary language.

The ELD standards may be used as criteria to develop the entry-level assessments and the assessments to monitor student progress called for in the *Reading/Language Arts Framework*.

English learners working at the advanced level of the ELD standards are to demonstrate proficiency in the English–language arts standards for their grade level and for all prior grade levels. This expectation means that English learners must acquire prerequisite skills at earlier proficiency levels.

Teachers are to monitor the students' acquisition of English and provide correction so that kindergarten students working at the advanced ELD level and students in all other grades working at the early advanced level will have internalized English-language skills to such a degree that the teacher will often observe the students correcting their own grammar, usage, and word choices in speaking, reading, and writing.

English-Language Development Standards

The ELD standards are designed to assist classroom teachers in assessing the progress of English learners toward attaining full fluency in English. The strategies used to help students attain proficiency in English differ according to the age at which a student begins learning English; therefore, the standards include outcomes for students who begin learning English in kindergarten through grade two, grades three through five, grades six through eight, and grades nine through twelve. The standards in those grade ranges were developed to help teachers move English learners to full fluency in English and to proficiency in the English–language arts standards. English learners at the advanced level of the ELD standards are to demonstrate proficiency in all standards detailed in this document and all language arts standards for the grades in which they are enrolled. English learners at the interme-diate level of these ELD standards should be able to demonstrate proficiency in the language arts standards for all prior grade levels. Teachers will need to work concurrently with this document and the *English–Language Arts Content Standards for California Public Schools, Kindergarten Through Grade Twelve* (1998) to ensure that English learners achieve proficiency.

The ELD standards are comprehensive, with more detailed proficiency levels than were included in the Executive Summary. This refinement is needed so that teachers can better assess the progress of their students. The proficiency levels are as follows:

- Beginning
- Early intermediate
- Intermediate
- Early advanced
- Advanced

Strategies and Applications

The listening and speaking standards for English learners identify a student's competency to understand the English language and to produce the language orally. Students must be prepared to use English effectively in social and academic settings. Listening and speaking skills provide one of the most important building blocks for the foundation of second-language acquisition and are essential for developing reading and writing skills in English. To develop proficiency in listening, speaking, reading, and writing, students must receive instruction in reading and writing while developing fluency in oral English.

Teachers must use both the ELD and the English–language arts standards to ensure that English learners develop proficiency in listening and speaking and acquire the concepts in the English–language arts standards. English learners achieving at the advanced level of the ELD standards should demonstrate proficiency in the language arts standards at their own grade level and at all prior grade levels. This expectation means that by the early advanced ELD level, all prerequisite skills needed to achieve the level of skills in the English–language arts standards must have been learned. English learners must develop both fluency in English and proficiency in the language arts standards. Teachers must ensure that English learners receive instruction in listening and speaking that will enable them to meet the speaking applications standards of the language arts standards.

Listening and Speaking

Strategies and Applications

English–language arts substrand	Beginning ELD level			
	Grades K–2	Grades 3–5	Grades 6–8	Grades 9–12
Comprehension	Begin to speak a few words or sentences by using some English phonemes and rudimentary English grammatical forms (e.g., single words or phrases).	Begin to speak a few words or sentences by using some English phonemes and rudimentary English grammatical forms (e.g., single words or phrases).	Begin to speak a few words or sentences by using some English phonemes and rudimentary English grammatical forms (e.g., single words or phrases).	Begin to speak a few words or sentences by using some English phonemes and rudimentary English grammatical forms (e.g., single words or phrases).
	Answer simple questions with one- to two-word responses.	Answer simple questions with one- to two-word responses.	Ask and answer questions by using simple sentences or phrases.	Ask and answer questions by using simple sentences or phrases.
	Respond to simple directions and questions by using physical actions and other means of nonverbal communication (e.g., matching objects, pointing to an answer, drawing pictures).	Retell familiar stories and participate in short conversations by using appropriate gestures, expressions, and illustrative objects.	Demonstrate comprehension of oral presentations and instructions through nonverbal responses (e.g., gestures, pointing, drawing).	Demonstrate comprehension of oral presentations and instructions through nonverbal responses.
Comprehension and Organization and Delivery of Oral Communication	Independently use common social greetings and simple repetitive phrases (e.g., "Thank you," "You're welcome").	Independently use common social greetings and simple repetitive phrases (e.g., "May I go and play?").	Independently use common social greetings and simple repetitive phrases (e.g., "Good morning, Ms. ___").	
Analysis and Evaluation of Oral and Media Communications and Comprehension				Respond with simple words or phrases to questions about simple written texts.
				Orally identify types of media (e.g., magazine, documentary film, news report).

Listening and Speaking

Strategies and Applications

English–language arts substrand	Early intermediate ELD level			
	Grades K–2	Grades 3–5	Grades 6–8	Grades 9–12
Comprehension	Begin to be understood when speaking but may have some inconsistent use of standard English grammatical forms and sounds (e.g., plurals, simple past tense, pronouns such as *he* or *she*).	Begin to be understood when speaking but may have some inconsistent use of standard English grammatical forms and sounds (e.g., plurals, simple past tense, pronouns such as *he* or *she*).	Begin to be understood when speaking but may have some inconsistent use of standard English grammatical forms and sounds (e.g., plurals, simple past tense, pronouns such as *he* or *she*).	Begin to be understood when speaking but may have some inconsistent use of standard English grammatical forms and sounds (e.g., plurals, simple past tense, pronouns such as *he* or *she*).
	Ask and answer questions by using phrases or simple sentences.	Ask and answer questions by using phrases or simple sentences.	Ask and answer questions by using phrases or simple sentences.	Ask and answer questions by using phrases or simple sentences.
		Restate and execute multiple-step oral directions.	Restate and execute multiple-step oral directions.	Restate and execute multiple-step oral directions.
Comprehension and Organization and Delivery of Oral Communication	Retell familiar stories and short conversations by using appropriate gestures, expressions, and illustrative objects.	Orally identify the main points of simple conversations and stories that are read aloud by using phrases or simple sentences.	Restate in simple sentences the main idea of oral presentations in subject-matter content.	Restate in simple sentences the main idea of oral presentations in subject-matter content.
	Orally communicate basic needs (e.g., "May I get a drink?").	Orally communicate basic needs (e.g., "May I get a drink of water?").	Orally communicate basic needs (e.g., "I need to borrow a pencil").	Orally communicate basic needs (e.g., "Do we have to _____?").
	Recite familiar rhymes, songs, and simple stories.	Recite familiar rhymes, songs, and simple stories.	Prepare and deliver short oral presentations.	Prepare and deliver short oral presentations.

Listening and Speaking

Strategies and Applications

English–language arts substrand	Intermediate ELD level			
	Grades K–2	Grades 3–5	Grades 6–8	Grades 9–12
Comprehension	Ask and answer instructional questions by using simple sentences.	Ask and answer instructional questions with some supporting elements (e.g., "Is it your turn to go to the computer lab?").	Respond to messages by asking simple questions or by briefly restating the message.	Respond to messages by asking simple questions or by briefly restating the message.
	Listen attentively to stories and information and identify important details and concepts by using both verbal and nonverbal responses.	Listen attentively to stories and information and identify important details and concepts by using both verbal and nonverbal responses.	Listen attentively to stories and information and identify important details and concepts by using both verbal and nonverbal responses.	Listen attentively to stories and information and identify important details and concepts by using both verbal and nonverbal responses.
Comprehension and Organization and Delivery of Oral Communication	Make oneself understood when speaking by using consistent standard English grammatical forms and sounds; however, some rules may not be followed (e.g., third-person singular, male and female pronouns).	Make oneself understood when speaking by using consistent standard English grammatical forms and sounds; however, some rules may not be followed (e.g., third-person singular, male and female pronouns).	Make oneself understood when speaking by using consistent standard English grammatical forms and sounds; however, some rules may not be followed (e.g., third-person singular, male and female pronouns).	Make oneself understood when speaking by using consistent standard English grammatical forms and sounds; however, some rules may not be followed (e.g., third-person singular, male and female pronouns).
	Participate in social conversations with peers and adults on familiar topics by asking and answering questions and soliciting information.	Participate in social conversations with peers and adults on familiar topics by asking and answering questions and soliciting information.	Participate in social conversations with peers and adults on familiar topics by asking and answering questions and soliciting information.	Participate in social conversations with peers and adults on familiar topics by asking and answering questions and soliciting information.
	Retell stories and talk about school-related activities by using expanded vocabulary, descriptive words, and paraphrasing.	Retell stories and talk about school-related activities by using expanded vocabulary, descriptive words, and paraphrasing.	Identify the main idea and some supporting details of oral presentations, familiar literature, and key concepts of subject-matter content.	Identify the main idea and some supporting details of oral presentations, familiar literature, and key concepts of subject-matter content.

(Continued on p. 20)

Listening and Speaking

Strategies and Applications

English–language arts substrand	Intermediate ELD level *(Continued)*			
	Grades K–2	Grades 3–5	Grades 6–8	Grades 9–12
Organization and Delivery of Oral Communication				Identify a variety of media messages (e.g., radio, television, movies) and give some details supporting the messages.
			Prepare and deliver short presentations on ideas, premises, or images obtained from various common sources.	Prepare and deliver short presentations on ideas, premises, or images obtained from various common sources.
				Prepare and ask basic interview questions and respond to them.

Listening and Speaking

Strategies and Applications

English–language arts substrand	Early advanced ELD level			
	Grades K–2	Grades 3–5	Grades 6–8	Grades 9–12
Comprehension	Listen attentively to stories and information and orally identify key details and concepts.	Listen attentively to more complex stories and information on new topics across content areas and identify the main points and supporting details.	Listen attentively to more complex stories and information on new topics across content areas and identify the main points and supporting details.	
Comprehension and Organization and Delivery of Oral Communication	Retell stories in greater detail by including the characters, setting, and plot.	Summarize major ideas and retell stories in greater detail by including the characters, setting, and plot.	Retell stories in greater detail by including the characters, setting, and plot.	Summarize literary pieces in greater detail by including the characters, setting, and plot and analyzing them in greater detail.
	Make oneself understood when speaking by using consistent standard English grammatical forms, sounds, intonation, pitch, and modulation but may make random errors.	Make oneself understood when speaking by using consistent standard English grammatical forms, sounds, intonation, pitch, and modulation but may make random errors.	Make oneself understood when speaking by using consistent standard English grammatical forms, sounds, intonation, pitch, and modulation but may make random errors.	Make oneself understood when speaking by using consistent standard English grammatical forms, sounds, intonation, pitch, and modulation but may make random errors.
	Participate in and initiate more extended social conversations with peers and adults on unfamiliar topics by asking and answering questions and restating and soliciting information.	Participate in and initiate more extended social conversations with peers and adults on unfamiliar topics by asking and answering questions and restating and soliciting information.	Participate in and initiate more extended social conversations with peers and adults on unfamiliar topics by asking and answering questions and restating and soliciting information.	Participate in and initiate more extended social conversations with peers and adults on unfamiliar topics by asking and answering questions and restating and soliciting information.
	Recognize appropriate ways of speaking that vary according to the purpose, audience, and subject matter.	Recognize appropriate ways of speaking that vary according to the purpose, audience, and subject matter.	Recognize appropriate ways of speaking that vary according to the purpose, audience, and subject matter.	Recognize appropriate ways of speaking that vary according to the purpose, audience, and subject matter.

(Continued on p. 22)

Listening and Speaking

Strategies and Applications

English–language arts substrand	Early advanced ELD level *(Continued)*			
	Grades K–2	Grades 3–5	Grades 6–8	Grades 9–12
Comprehension and Organization and Delivery of Oral Communication	Ask and answer instructional questions with more extensive supporting elements (e.g., "Which part of the story was the most important?").	Ask and answer instructional questions with more extensive supporting elements (e.g., "Which part of the story was the most important?").	Respond to messages by asking questions, challenging statements, or offering examples that affirm the message.	Respond to messages by asking questions, challenging statements, or offering examples that affirm the message.
		Use simple figurative language and idiomatic expressions (e.g., "It's raining cats and dogs") to communicate ideas to a variety of audiences.	Use simple figurative language and idiomatic expressions (e.g., "heavy as a ton of bricks," "soaking wet") to communicate ideas to a variety of audiences.	Use simple figurative language and idiomatic expressions (e.g., "sunshine girl," "heavy as a ton of bricks") to communicate ideas to a variety of audiences.
			Prepare and deliver presentations that use various sources.	Prepare and deliver presentations that follow a process of organization and use various sources.
				Prepare and deliver brief oral presentations/reports on historical investigations, a problem and solution, or a cause and effect.

Listening and Speaking

Strategies and Applications

English–language arts substrand	Advanced ELD level			
	Grades K–2	Grades 3–5	Grades 6–8	Grades 9–12
Comprehension	Listen attentively to stories and information on new topics and identify both orally and in writing key details and concepts.	Listen attentively to stories and information on topics; identify the main points and supporting details.	Listen attentively to stories and information on topics; identify the main points and supporting details.	
	Demonstrate an understanding of idiomatic expressions (e.g., "Give me a hand") by responding to such expressions and using them appropriately.	Demonstrate an understanding of idiomatic expressions (e.g., "It's pouring outside") by responding to such expressions and using them appropriately.	Demonstrate an understanding of figurative language and idiomatic expressions by responding to such expressions and using them appropriately.	Demonstrate an understanding of figurative language and idiomatic expressions by responding to such expressions and using them appropriately.
				Identify strategies used by the media to present information for various purposes (e.g., to inform, entertain, or persuade).
Comprehension and Organization and Delivery of Oral Communication	Negotiate and initiate social conversations by questioning, restating, soliciting information, and paraphrasing the communication of others.	Negotiate and initiate social conversations by questioning, restating, soliciting information, and paraphrasing the communication of others.	Negotiate and initiate social conversations by questioning, restating, soliciting information, and paraphrasing the communication of others.	Negotiate and initiate social conversations by questioning, restating, soliciting information, and paraphrasing the communication of others.
	Consistently use appropriate ways of speaking and writing that vary according to the purpose, audience, and subject matter.	Consistently use appropriate ways of speaking and writing that vary according to the purpose, audience, and subject matter.	Consistently use appropriate ways of speaking and writing that vary according to the purpose, audience, and subject matter.	Consistently use appropriate ways of speaking and writing that vary according to the purpose, audience, and subject matter.

(Continued on p. 24)

Listening and Speaking

Strategies and Applications

English–language arts substrand	Advanced ELD level *(Continued)*			
	Grades K–2	Grades 3–5	Grades 6–8	Grades 9–12
Comprehension and Organization and Delivery of Oral Communication	Narrate and paraphrase events in greater detail by using more extended vocabulary.	Identify the main ideas and points of view and distinguish fact from fiction in broadcast and print media.	Prepare and deliver presentations and reports in various content areas, including a purpose, point of view, introduction, coherent transition, and appropriate conclusions.	Prepare and deliver presentations and reports in various content areas, including a purpose, point of view, introduction, coherent transition, and appropriate conclusions.
	Speak clearly and comprehensibly by using standard English grammatical forms, sounds, intonation, pitch, and modulation.	Speak clearly and comprehensibly by using standard English grammatical forms, sounds, intonation, pitch, and modulation.	Speak clearly and comprehensibly by using standard English grammatical forms, sounds, intonation, pitch, and modulation.	Speak clearly and comprehensibly by using standard English grammatical forms, sounds, intonation, pitch, and modulation.

Word Analysis

For all students, developing skills in reading English begins with a solid understanding of the relationships between English sounds and letters—the relationships between the spoken and written language. For the English learner those concepts are first developed through the recognition and production of English sounds. Students need to learn first those sounds that exist and then those that do not exist in their first language. Students then are taught to transfer this knowledge to the printed language. As students develop knowledge of the correspondence between sounds and printed symbols, they also develop skills to deal with English morphemes (e.g., prefixes, suffixes, root words). Those word-analysis skills are some of the building blocks students need to develop fluency in English and literacy skills.

Native speakers of English are expected to recognize and produce all the English sounds by no later than first grade. This knowledge is then used in phonics instruction when children learn to match the English sounds with printed letters and use this knowledge to decode and encode words. English learners in kindergarten through grade two are to demonstrate proficiency in those English–language arts standards pertaining to phonemic awareness, concepts about print, and decoding standards appropriate for their grade levels by the time they reach the advanced level of the ELD standards.

Because the English–language arts standards are essential for all students learning to read in English, English learners in grades three through twelve should be proficient in those standards related to phonemic awareness, concepts about print, and decoding no later than at the early intermediate level. Except where it is necessary for instruction to use nonsense words for teaching and assessing students, such as in phonemic awareness and early decoding instruction, care should be taken to ensure that students work with vocabulary and concepts that are meaningful and understandable to them.

For kindergarten through grade two, the English–language arts standards pertaining to phonemic awareness, concepts about print, and decoding/word recognition have been incorporated into the ELD standards. Those language arts standards serve as signs of whether English learners are making appropriate progress toward becoming proficient readers. The ELD standards indicate the grade span in which students are to demonstrate proficiency, the language arts substrand, and the number of the targeted language arts standard. Nonreaders of any age must move through the same sequence of skills when learning to read. Therefore, the instructional sequence for kindergarten through grade two should be used as a guide for English-language development and reading instruction at all grade levels.

The instructional sequence for teaching phonemic awareness, concepts about print, and decoding skills is more specific in the kindergarten-through-grade-two span because the language arts standards for those grades focus primarily on developing literacy fluency. In grades three through twelve, students must greatly increase their content knowledge while learning English literacy skills. Older students with properly sequenced instruction may achieve literacy more rapidly than very young children do.

In the ELD standards pathways are provided that enable students of all ages to build literacy skills. The language arts standards for grades three through twelve have linking ELD standards in each grade span that are designed to help students achieve proficiency in their grade-level language arts standards by the time they reach the advanced level of the ELD standards. Students at the advanced level in ELD are expected to demonstrate proficiency in the language arts standards for their own grade and for all prior grades.

One reason for incorporating the language arts standards for kindergarten through grade two into the ELD standards is to clarify a point: Kindergarten and first-grade students at the advanced level in the ELD standards are also expected to be proficient in the language arts standards for their grade level. No limited-English-proficient student is expected to learn the language arts standards beyond his or her grade level.

Reading

Word Analysis

English–language arts substrand	Beginning ELD level			
	Grades K–2	Grades 3–5	Grades 6–8	Grades 9–12
Concepts About Print, Phonemic Awareness, and Vocabulary and Concept Development	Recognize English phonemes that correspond to phonemes students already hear and produce in their primary language.	Recognize English phonemes that correspond to phonemes students already hear and produce while reading aloud.	Recognize and correctly pronounce most English phonemes while reading aloud.	Recognize and correctly pronounce most English phonemes while reading aloud.
Phonemic Awareness and Decoding and Word Recognition		Recognize sound/symbol relationships in one's own writing.	Recognize the most common English morphemes in phrases and simple sentences.	Recognize the most common English morphemes in phrases and simple sentences (e.g., basic syllabication rules, phonics, regular and irregular plurals).

Reading

Word Analysis

English–language arts substrand	Early intermediate ELD level			
	Grades K–2	Grades 3–5	Grades 6–8	Grades 9–12
Concepts About Print, Phonemic Awareness, and Vocabulary and Concept Development	Produce English phonemes that correspond to phonemes students already hear and produce, including long and short vowels and initial and final consonants. ***English–Language Arts Content Standards*** **Kindergarten: Phonemic Awareness** 1.7 Track (move sequentially from sound to sound) and represent the number, sameness/difference, and order of two and three isolated phonemes (e.g., /f, s, th/,/j, d, j/). 1.10 Identify and produce rhyming words in response to an oral prompt. **Grade One: Phonemic Awareness** 1.4 Distinguish initial, medial, and final sounds in single-syllable words.	While reading aloud, recognize and produce English phonemes that do not correspond to phonemes students already hear and produce (e.g., *a* in *cat* and final consonants).	Produce most English phonemes comprehensibly while reading aloud one's own writing, simple sentences, or simple texts.	Produce most English phonemes comprehensibly while reading aloud one's own writing, simple sentences, or simple texts.
	Recognize English phonemes that do not correspond to sounds students hear and produce, (e.g., *a* in *cat* and final consonants). ***English–Language Arts Content Standards*** **Kindergarten: Phonemic Awareness** 1.7 Track (move sequentially from sound to sound) and represent the number, sameness/difference, and order of two and three isolated phonemes (e.g., /f, s, th/,/j,d,j/). 1.10 Identify and produce rhyming words in response to an oral prompt. **Grade One: Phonemic Awareness** 1.4 Distinguish initial, medial, and final sounds in single-syllable words.			

(Continued on p. 29)

Reading

Word Analysis

English–language arts substrand	Early intermediate ELD level *(Continued)*			
	Grades K–2	Grades 3–5	Grades 6–8	Grades 9–12
Decoding and Word Recognition and Vocabulary and Concept Development		Recognize common English morphemes in phrases and simple sentences (e.g., basic syllabication rules and phonics).	Use common English morphemes in oral and silent reading	Use common English morphemes in oral and silent reading.
			Recognize obvious cognates (e.g., *education, educación; university, universidad*) in phrases, simple sentences, literature, and content area texts.	Recognize obvious cognates (e.g., *education, educación; university, universidad*) in phrases, simple sentences, literature, and content area texts.

Reading

Word Analysis

English–language arts substrand	Intermediate ELD level			
	Grades K–2	Grades 3–5	Grades 6–8	Grades 9–12
Phonemic Awareness	Pronounce most English phonemes correctly while reading aloud. ***English–Language Arts Content Standards*** **Kindergarten: Phonemic Awareness** 1.7 Track (move sequentially from sound to sound) and represent the number, sameness/difference, and order of two and three isolated phonemes (e.g., */f, s, th/,/j, d, j/*). **Grade One: Phonemic Awareness** 1.5 Distinguish long- and short-vowel sounds in orally stated single-syllable words (e.g., *bit/bite*). 1.6 Create and say a series of rhyming words, including consonant blends. 1.7 Add, delete, or change target sounds to change words (e.g., change *cow* to *how; pan* to *an*). 1.8 Blend two to four phonemes into recognizable words (e.g., */c/a/t/ = cat; /f/l/a/t/ = flat*). 1.9 Segment single syllable words into their components (e.g., */c/a/t/ = cat; /s/p/l/a/t/ = splat; /r/i/ch/ = rich*).	Pronounce most English phonemes correctly while reading aloud.		
Decoding and Word Recognition	Recognize sound/symbol relationships and basic word-formation rules in phrases, simple sentences, or simple text. ***English–Language Arts Content Standards*** **Grade Two: Decoding and Word Recognition** 1.4 Recognize common abbreviations (e.g., *Jan., Sun., Mr., St.*).	Use common English morphemes in oral and silent reading.	Apply knowledge of common English morphemes in oral and silent reading to derive meaning from literature and texts in content areas.	Apply knowledge of common English morphemes in oral and silent reading to derive meaning from literature and texts in content areas.

(Continued on p. 31)

Reading

Word Analysis

English–language arts substrand	Intermediate ELD level *(Continued)*			
	Grades K–2	Grades 3–5	Grades 6–8	Grades 9–12
Decoding and Word Recognition			Identify cognates (e.g., *agonía, agony*) and false cognates (e.g., *éxito, success*) in literature and texts in content areas.	Identify cognates (e.g., *agonía, agony*) and false cognates (e.g., *éxito, success*) in literature and texts in content areas.
Concepts About Print	Recognize and name all uppercase and lowercase letters of the alphabet. ***English–Language Arts Content Standards*** **Kindergarten** 1.1 Identify the front cover, back cover, and title page of a book. 1.2 Follow words from left to right and from top to bottom on the printed page. 1.3 Understand that printed materials provide information. 1.4 Recognize that sentences in print are made up of separate words. 1.5 Distinguish letters from words. **Grade One** 1.1 Match spoken words to printed words. 1.3 Identify letters, words, and sentences.			

Reading

Word Analysis

English–language arts substrand	Early advanced ELD level			
	Grades K–2	Grades 3–5	Grades 6–8	Grades 9–12
Phonemic Awareness and Decoding and Word Recognition	Use common English morphemes to derive meaning in oral and silent reading (e.g., basic syllabication rules, regular and irregular plurals, and basic phonics). ***English–Language Arts Content Standards*** **Kindergarten: Phonemic Awareness** 1.8 Track (move sequentially from sound to sound) and represent changes in simple syllables and words with two and three sounds as one sound is added, substituted, omitted, shifted, or repeated (e.g., vowel-consonant, consonant-vowel, or consonant-vowel-consonant). 1.9 Blend vowel-consonant sounds orally to make words or syllables. 1.11 Distinguish orally stated one-syllable words and separate into beginning or ending sounds. 1.12 Track auditorily each word in a sentence and each syllable in a word. 1.13 Count the number of sounds in syllables and syllables in words.	Apply knowledge of common English morphemes in oral and silent reading to derive meaning from literature and texts in content areas.	Apply knowledge of word relationships, such as roots and affixes, to derive meaning from literature and texts in content areas.	Apply knowledge of word relationships, such as roots and affixes, to derive meaning from literature and texts in content areas (e.g., *remove, extend*).
	Grade Two 1.1 Recognize and use knowledge of spelling patterns (e.g., diphthongs, special vowel spellings) when reading. 1.2 Apply knowledge of basic syllabication rules when reading (e.g., vowel-consonant-vowel = *su/per*; vowel-consonant/ consonant-vowel = *sup/ per*). 1.3 Decode two-syllable nonsense words and regular multisyllabic words. 1.5 Identify and correctly use regular plurals (e.g., *-s, -es, -ies*) and irregular plurals (e.g., *fly/flies, wife/wives*). 1.6 Read aloud fluently and accurately and with appropriate intonation and expression.			

(Continued on p. 33)

Reading

Word Analysis

English–language arts substrand	Early advanced ELD level *(Continued)*			
	Grades K–2	Grades 3–5	Grades 6–8	Grades 9–12
Phonemic Awareness and Decoding and Word Recognition	Recognize sound/symbol relationship and basic word-formation rules in phrases, simple sentences, or simple text. *English–Language Arts Content Standards* **Kindergarten: Decoding and Word Recognition** 1.14 Match all consonant and short-vowel sounds to appropriate letters. 1.15 Read simple one-syllable and high-frequency words (i.e., sight words). 1.16 Understand that as letters of words change, so do the sounds (i.e., the alphabetic principle).		Distinguish between cognates and false cognates in literature and texts in content areas.	Distinguish between cognates and false cognates in literature and texts in content areas.
	Grade One: Decoding and Word Recognition 1.10 Generate the sounds from all the letters and letter patterns, including consonant blends and long- and short-vowel patterns (i.e., phonograms), and blend those sounds into recognizable words. 1.11 Read common, irregular sight words (e.g., *the, have, said, come, give, of*). 1.12 Use knowledge of vowel digraphs and *r*-controlled letter-sound associations to read words. 1.13 Read compound words and contractions. 1.14 Read inflectional forms (e.g., *-s, -ed, -ing*) and root words (e.g., *look, looked, looking*). 1.15 Read common word families (e.g., *-ite, -ate*). 1.16 Read aloud with fluency in a manner that sounds like natural speech.			

Reading

Word Analysis

English–language arts substrand	Advanced ELD level			
	Grades K–2	Grades 3–5	Grades 6–8	Grades 9–12
Decoding and Word Recognition	Apply knowledge of common morphemes to derive meaning in oral and silent reading (e.g., basic syllabication rules, regular and irregular plurals, and basic phonics). ***English–Language Arts Content Standards*** **Kindergarten** 1.14 Match all consonant and short-vowel sounds to appropriate letters. 1.15 Read simple one-syllable and high-frequency words (i.e., sight words). 1.16 Understand that as letters of words change, so do the sounds (i.e., the alphabetic principle). **Grade One** 1.10 Generate the sounds from all the letters and letter patterns, including consonant blends and long- and short-vowel patterns (i.e., phonograms), and blend those sounds into recognizable words. 1.11 Read common, irregular sight words (e.g., *the, have, said, come, give, of*). 1.12 Use knowledge of vowel digraphs and *r*-controlled letter-sound associations to read words. 1.13 Read compound words and contractions. 1.14 Read inflectional forms (e.g., *-s, -ed, -ing*) and root words (e.g., *look, looked, looking*). 1.15 Read common word families (e.g., *-ite, -ate*). 1.16 Read aloud with fluency in a manner that sounds like natural speech.	Apply knowledge of word relationships, such as roots and affixes, to derive meaning from literature and texts in content areas.	Apply knowledge of word relationships, such as roots and affixes, to derive meaning from literature and texts in content areas.	Apply knowledge of word relationships, such as roots and affixes, to derive meaning from literature and texts in content areas.

(Continued on p. 35)

Reading

Word Analysis

English–language arts substrand	Advanced ELD level *(Continued)*			
	Grades K–2	Grades 3–5	Grades 6–8	Grades 9–12
Decoding and Word Recognition	**Grade Two** 1.1 Recognize and use knowledge of spelling patterns (e.g., diphthongs, special vowel spellings) when reading. 1.2 Apply knowledge of basic syllabication rules when reading (e.g., vowel-consonant-vowel = *su/per*; vowel-consonant/consonant-vowel = *sup/per*). 1.3 Decode two-syllable nonsense words and regular multisyllable words. 1.4 Recognize common abbreviations (e.g., *Jan., Sun., Mr., St.*). 1.5 Identify and correctly use regular plurals (e.g., *-s, -es, -ies*) and irregular plurals (e.g., *fly/flies, wife/wives*).			
			Apply knowledge of cognates and false cognates to derive meaning from literature and texts in content areas.	Apply knowledge of cognates and false cognates to derive meaning from literature and texts in content areas.

Fluency and Systematic Vocabulary Development

As the English learner recognizes and produces the sounds of English, the student is simultaneously building vocabulary. Learning new labels for concepts, objects, and actions is a key building block for the integration of the language. The pathways in the English-language development (ELD) standards lead to the achievement of fluent oral and silent reading. Those pathways are created by building vocabulary and are demonstrated through actions and spoken words, phrases, and sentences and by transferring this understanding to reading. The successful learning of a second language requires that the instruction of students be highly integrated to include all language skills and challenging activities that focus on subject-matter content (Brinton, Snow, and Wesche 1989). Therefore, at the higher proficiency levels, the student is asked to apply knowledge of vocabulary to literature and subject-matter texts and achieve an appropriate level of independent reading.

At the lower ELD proficiency levels, reading materials should be at the student's developmental level. Grade-level reading materials should be used with students working at the advanced level. In addition to demonstrating proficiency in the ELD standards, students at the advanced level must also demonstrate proficiency in the English–language arts standards at their own grade level and at all prior grade levels. To ensure each student's success, schools must offer instruction leading to proficiency in the language arts standards. Instruction must begin as early as possible within the framework of the ELD standards. To ensure that all English learners achieve proficiency in the language arts standards, teachers must concurrently use both documents: the English–language arts standards and the ELD standards.

Reading

Fluency and Systematic Vocabulary Development

English–language arts substrand	Beginning ELD level			
	Grades K–2	Grades 3–5	Grades 6–8	Grades 9–12
Vocabulary and Concept Development				Recognize simple affixes (e.g., *educate, education*), prefixes (e.g., *dislike*), synonyms (e.g., *big, large*), and antonyms (e.g., *hot, cold*).
	Read aloud simple words (e.g., nouns and adjectives) in stories or games. ***English–Language Arts Content Standards* Kindergarten** 1.17 Identify and sort common words in basic categories (e.g., colors, shapes, foods).	Read aloud simple words (e.g., nouns and adjectives) in stories or games.	Read aloud simple words presented in literature and subject-matter texts; demonstrate comprehension by using one to two words or simple-sentence responses.	Read aloud simple words presented in literature and subject-matter texts; demonstrate comprehension by using one to two words or simple-sentence responses.
	Respond appropriately to some social and academic interactions (e.g., simple question/answer, negotiate play).	Respond appropriately to some social and academic interactions (e.g., simple question/answer, negotiate play).	Respond with appropriate short phrases or sentences in various social and academic settings (e.g., answer simple questions).	Respond with appropriate short phrases or sentences in various social and academic settings (e.g., answer simple questions).
			Create a simple dictionary of words frequently used by the student.	Use an English dictionary to find the meaning of simple known vocabulary.

(Continued on p. 38)

Reading

Fluency and Systematic Vocabulary Development

English–language arts substrand	Beginning ELD level *(Continued)*			
	Grades K–2	Grades 3–5	Grades 6–8	Grades 9–12
Vocabulary and Concept Development *(The standards are also addressed in "Listening and Speaking.")*	Demonstrate comprehension of simple vocabulary with an appropriate action.	Demonstrate comprehension of simple vocabulary with an appropriate action.		
	Retell simple stories by using drawings, words, or phrases.	Retell simple stories by using drawings, words, or phrases.	Retell stories by using phrases and sentences.	
	Produce simple vocabulary (single words or short phrases) to communicate basic needs in social and academic settings (e.g., locations, greetings, classroom objects).	Produce simple vocabulary (single words or short phrases) to communicate basic needs in social and academic settings (e.g., locations, greetings, classroom objects).	Produce simple vocabulary (single words or short phrases) to communicate basic needs in social and academic settings (e.g., locations, greetings, classroom objects).	Produce simple vocabulary (single words or short phrases) to communicate basic needs in social and academic settings (e.g., locations, greetings, classroom objects).

Reading

Fluency and Systematic Vocabulary Development

English–language arts substrand	Early intermediate ELD level			
	Grades K–2	Grades 3–5	Grades 6–8	Grades 9–12
Vocabulary and Concept Development	Produce vocabulary, phrases, and simple sentences to communicate basic needs in social and academic settings.	Apply knowledge of content-related vocabulary to discussions and reading.	Use knowledge of literature and content areas to understand unknown words.	Begin to use knowledge of simple affixes, prefixes, synonyms, and antonyms to interpret the meaning of unknown words.
				Recognize simple idioms, analogies, and figures of speech (e.g., "the last word") in literature and subject-matter texts.
	Read simple vocabulary, phrases, and sentences independently.	Read simple vocabulary, phrases, and sentences independently.	Read simple paragraphs and passages independently.	Read simple paragraphs and passages independently.
				Recognize that some words have multiple meanings and apply this knowledge to texts.
	Read aloud an increasing number of English words.	Use knowledge of English morphemes, phonics, and syntax to decode and interpret the meaning of unfamiliar words in simple sentences.		
	Demonstrate internalization of English grammar, usage, and word choice by recognizing and correcting some errors when speaking or reading aloud.*	Demonstrate internalization of English grammar, usage, and word choice by recognizing and correcting some errors when speaking or reading aloud.*	Demonstrate internalization of English grammar, usage, and word choice by recognizing and correcting some errors when speaking or reading aloud.*	Demonstrate internalization of English grammar, usage, and word choice by recognizing and correcting some errors when speaking or reading aloud.*

*Teachers are to monitor English learners' acquisition of English and provide correction so that kindergarten students working at the advanced ELD level and students in all other grades working at the early advanced level will have internalized English-language skills to such a degree that the teacher will often observe the students correcting their own grammar, usage, and word choices in speaking, reading, and writing.

(Continued on p. 40)

Reading

Fluency and Systematic Vocabulary Development

English–language arts substrand	Early intermediate ELD level *(Continued)*			
	Grades K–2	Grades 3–5	Grades 6–8	Grades 9–12
Vocabulary and Concept Development		Read aloud with some pacing, intonation, and expression one's own writing of narrative and expository texts.	Read aloud with appropriate pacing, intonation, and expression one's own writing of narrative and expository texts.	Read aloud with appropriate pacing, intonation, and expression one's own writing of narrative and expository texts.
			Use a standard dictionary to find the meaning of known vocabulary.	Use a standard dictionary to find the meaning of unknown vocabulary.
				Use appropriate connectors (e.g., *first, then, after that, finally*) to sequence written text.

Reading

Fluency and Systematic Vocabulary Development

English–language arts substrand	Intermediate ELD level			
	Grades K–2	Grades 3–5	Grades 6–8	Grades 9–12
Vocabulary and Concept Development		Create a simple dictionary of frequently used words.	Use a standard dictionary to determine meanings of unknown words.	Use a standard dictionary to derive the meaning of unknown vocabulary.
		Use knowledge of English morphemes, phonics, and syntax to decode and interpret the meaning of unfamiliar words in text.	Use knowledge of English morphemes, phonics, and syntax to decode text.	Identify variations of the same word that are found in a text and know with some accuracy how affixes change the meaning of those words.
			Recognize simple idioms, analogies, figures of speech (e.g., to "take a fall"), and metaphors in literature and texts in content areas.	Demonstrate sufficient knowledge of English syntax to interpret the meaning of idioms, analogies, and metaphors.
	Demonstrate internalization of English grammar, usage, and word choice by recognizing and correcting errors when speaking or reading aloud.*	Demonstrate internalization of English grammar, usage, and word choice by recognizing and correcting errors when speaking or reading aloud.*	Demonstrate internalization of English grammar, usage, and word choice by recognizing and correcting errors when speaking or reading aloud.*	Demonstrate internalization of English grammar, usage, and word choice by recognizing and correcting errors when speaking or reading aloud.*
	Use decoding skills to read more complex words independently. ***English–Language Arts Content Standards* Grade One** 1.17 Classify grade-appropriate categories of words (e.g., concrete collections of animals, foods, toys).	Read grade-appropriate narrative and expository texts aloud with appropriate pacing, intonation, and expression.		

*Teachers are to monitor English learners' acquisition of English and provide correction so that kindergarten students working at the advanced ELD level and students in all other grades working at the early advanced level will have internalized English-language skills to such a degree that the teacher will often observe the students correcting their own grammar, usage, and word choices in speaking, reading, and writing.

(Continued on p. 42)

Reading

Fluency and Systematic Vocabulary Development

English–language arts substrand	Intermediate ELD level *(Continued)*			
	Grades K–2	Grades 3–5	Grades 6–8	Grades 9–12
Vocabulary and Concept Development *(The standards are also addressed in "Listening and Speaking.")*	Use more complex vocabulary and sentences to communicate needs and express ideas in a wider variety of social and academic settings (e.g., classroom discussions, mediation of conflicts). ***English–Language Arts Content Standards*** **Kindergarten** 1.18 Describe common objects and events in both general and specific language.	Use content-related vocabulary in discussions and reading.	Use decoding skills and knowledge of both academic and social vocabulary to read independently.	Use decoding skills and knowledge of both academic and social vocabulary to read independently.
	Apply knowledge of content-related vocabulary to discussions and reading.			
Vocabulary and Concept Development and Decoding and Word Recognition	Recognize simple prefixes and suffixes when they are attached to known vocabulary (e.g., *remove, jumping*).	Recognize some common root words and affixes when they are attached to known vocabulary (e.g., *speak, speaker*).	Recognize that some words have multiple meanings.	Apply knowledge of text connectors to make inferences.

Reading

Fluency and Systematic Vocabulary Development

English–language arts substrand	Early advanced ELD level			
	Grades K–2	Grades 3–5	Grades 6–8	Grades 9–12
Vocabulary and Concept Development		Use knowledge of English morphemes, phonics, and syntax to decode and interpret the meaning of unfamiliar words.	Use knowledge of English morphemes, phonics, and syntax to decode and interpret the meaning of unfamiliar words.	Use knowledge of English morphemes, phonics, and syntax to decode and interpret the meaning of unfamiliar words.
	Recognize simple antonyms and synonyms (e.g., *good, bad; blend, mix*) in stories or games.	Recognize that some words have multiple meanings (e.g., *present/gift, present/time*) in literature and texts in content areas.	Recognize that some words have multiple meanings and apply this knowledge to read literature and texts in content areas.	Recognize that some words have multiple meanings and apply this knowledge to understand texts.
	Use simple prefixes and suffixes when they are attached to known vocabulary. ***English–Language Arts Content Standards*** **Grade Two** 1.9 Know the meaning of simple prefixes and suffixes (e.g., *over-, un-, -ing, -ly*).	Use some common root words and affixes when they are attached to known vocabulary (e.g., *educate, education*).		Use knowledge of affixes, root words, and increased vocabulary to interpret the meaning of words in literature and content area texts.
		Use a standard dictionary to find the meaning of known vocabulary.	Use a standard dictionary to determine the meaning of unknown words (e.g., idioms and words with multiple meanings).	Use a standard dictionary to determine the meaning of unknown words (e.g., idioms and words with multiple meanings).
		Recognize simple analogies (e.g., "fly like a bird") and metaphors used in literature and texts in content areas.		

(Continued on p. 44)

Reading

Fluency and Systematic Vocabulary Development

English–language arts substrand	Early advanced ELD level *(Continued)*			
	Grades K–2	Grades 3–5	Grades 6–8	Grades 9–12
Vocabulary and Concept Development	Use decoding skills and knowledge of academic and social vocabulary to begin independent reading.	Use decoding skills and knowledge of academic and social vocabulary to achieve independent reading.	Use decoding skills and knowledge of academic and social vocabulary to achieve independent reading.	Use decoding skills and knowledge of academic and social vocabulary to achieve independent reading.
		Recognize some common idioms (e.g., "scared silly") in discussions and reading.	Recognize idioms, analogies, and metaphors used in literature and texts in content areas.	Recognize idioms, analogies, and metaphors used in literature and texts in content areas.
		Read aloud with appropriate pacing, intonation, and expression increasingly complex narrative and expository texts.	Read aloud with appropriate pacing, intonation, and expression increasingly complex narrative and expository texts.	Read aloud with appropriate pacing, intonation, and expression increasingly complex narrative and expository texts.

Reading

Fluency and Systematic Vocabulary Development

English–language arts substrand	Advanced ELD level			
	Grades K–2	Grades 3–5	Grades 6–8	Grades 9–12
Vocabulary and Concept Development	Explain common antonyms and synonyms. ***English–Language Arts Content Standards*** **Grade Two** 1.7 Understand and explain common antonyms and synonyms.	Apply knowledge of common root words and affixes when they are attached to known vocabulary.		
	Recognize words that have multiple meanings in texts. ***English–Language Arts Content Standards*** **Grade Two** 1.10 Identify simple multiple-meaning words.	Recognize that some words have multiple meanings and apply this knowledge consistently.	Recognize that some words have multiple meanings and apply this knowledge consistently in reading literature and texts in content areas.	Recognize that some words have multiple meanings and apply this knowledge consistently in reading literature and texts in content areas.
	Apply knowledge of academic and social vocabulary to achieve independent reading. ***English–Language Arts Content Standards*** **Grade Two** 1.8 Use knowledge of individual words in unknown compound words to predict their meaning.	Apply knowledge of academic and social vocabulary to achieve independent reading.	Apply knowledge of academic and social vocabulary to achieve independent reading.	Apply knowledge of academic and social vocabulary to achieve independent reading.
		Use common idioms, some analogies, and metaphors in discussion and reading.	Use common idioms and some analogies (e.g., "shine like a star," "let the cat out of the bag") and metaphors.	Use common idioms and some analogies (e.g., "shine like a star," "let the cat out of the bag") and metaphors.
		Use a standard dictionary to determine the meaning of unknown words.	Use a standard dictionary to determine the meaning of unknown words.	Use a standard dictionary to determine the meaning of unknown words.

(Continued on p. 46)

Reading

Fluency and Systematic Vocabulary Development

English–language arts substrand	Advanced ELD level *(Continued)*			
	Grades K–2	Grades 3–5	Grades 6–8	Grades 9–12
Vocabulary and Concept Development	Read aloud with appropriate pacing, intonation, and expression narrative and expository texts.	Read aloud with appropriate pacing, intonation, and expression narrative and expository texts.		
Decoding and Word Recognition	***English–Language Arts Content Standards*** **Kindergarten** 1.14 Match all consonant and short-vowel sounds to appropriate letters. 1.15 Read simple one-syllable and high-frequency words (i.e., sight words). 1.16 Understand that as letters change, so do the sounds (i.e., the alphabetic principle). **Grade One** 1.10 Generate the sounds from all the letters and letter patterns, including consonant blends and long- and short-vowel patterns (i.e., phonograms), and blend those sounds into recognizable words. 1.11 Read common, irregular sight words (e.g., *the, have, said, come, give, of*). 1.12 Use knowledge of vowel digraphs and *r*-controlled letter-sound associations to read words. 1.13 Read compound words and contractions. 1.14 Read inflectional forms (e.g., *-s, -ed, -ing*) and root words (e.g., *look, looked, looking*). 1.15 Read common word families (e.g., *-ite, -ate*). 1.16 Read aloud with fluency in a manner that sounds like natural speech.			

(Continued on p. 47)

Reading

Fluency and Systematic Vocabulary Development

English–language arts substrand	Advanced ELD level (Continued)			
	Grades K–2	Grades 3–5	Grades 6–8	Grades 9–12
Decoding and Word Recognition	**Grade Two** 1.1 Recognize and use knowledge of spelling patterns (e.g., diphthongs, special vowel spellings) when reading. 1.2 Apply knowledge of basic syllabication rules when reading (e.g., vowel-consonant-vowel = *su/per*; vowel-consonant/consonant-vowel = *sup/per*). 1.3 Decode two-syllable nonsense words and regular multisyllable words. 1.4 Recognize common abbreviations (e.g., *Jan., Sun., Mr., St.*). 1.5 Identify and correctly use regular plurals (e.g., *-s, -es, -ies*) and irregular plurals (e.g., *fly/flies, wife/wives*)			

Reading Comprehension

Reading comprehension and literary response and analysis are the two pathways of the ELD standards that lead to mastery of the academic content of the language arts standards. The English learner requires instruction in which listening, speaking, reading, and writing are presented in an integrated format. The ELD standards vary according to the grade level and the age of the student: early childhood (ages five to seven years), middle childhood (ages eight to ten years), and young adult (ages eleven to sixteen years). The speed of acquisition of academic language in English differs within those three groups (Collier 1992). Older children and adults, over the short term, proceed more quickly through the very early stages of syntactical and morphological development (Scarcella and Oxford 1992). Young children proceed less quickly, but in the long run they achieve higher levels of proficiency in a second language than do older children and adults. The influence of age is most evident with younger children who are able to learn a second language and speak that language with nativelike fluency and pronunciation (Selinker 1972). Younger children exhibit few of the inappropriate (e.g., phonological, syntactical, or morphological) forms of the second language that often are problematic for older children and adults and that require extensive remediation.

When English learners reach the advanced level of the ELD standards, they must also be able to demonstrate proficiency in the language arts standards for their current grade level and all prior grade levels. Students at the advanced level of the ELD standards must use grade-level texts; however, students working at lower levels should use reading materials appropriate for their developmental levels. To ensure that English learners become proficient in both the ELD and the language arts standards, teachers must use the two standards documents concurrently and provide instruction leading to proficiency in the language arts standards at a level no later than the intermediate level of the ELD standards.

Reading

Reading Comprehension

English–language arts substrand	Beginning ELD level			
	Grades K–2	Grades 3–5	Grades 6–8	Grades 9–12
Comprehension	Respond orally to stories read aloud, using physical actions and other means of nonverbal communication (e.g., matching objects, pointing to an answer, drawing pictures).			
	Respond orally to stories read aloud, giving one- or two-word responses (e.g., "brown bear") to factual comprehension questions.	Respond orally to stories read aloud by giving one- or two-word responses (e.g., "brown bear") to factual comprehension questions.	Read simple text and orally respond to factual comprehension questions by using key words or phrases.	
	Draw pictures from one's own experience related to a story or topic (e.g., community in social studies).	Orally identify the relationship between simple text read aloud and one's own experience by using key words and/or phrases.		
	Understand and follow simple one-step directions for classroom activities.	Understand and follow simple one-step directions for classroom activities.	Understand and follow simple multiple-step oral directions for classroom or work-related activities.	Understand and follow simple multiple-step oral directions for classroom or work-related activities.
Comprehension and Analysis of Grade-Level-Appropriate Text	Identify, using key words or pictures, the basic sequence of events in stories read aloud.	Identify, using key words or pictures, the basic sequence of events in stories read aloud.	Recognize categories of common informational materials (e.g., newspaper, brochure).	Recognize a few specific facts in familiar expository texts, such as consumer publications, workplace documents, and content area texts.

(Continued on p. 50)

Reading

Reading Comprehension

English–language arts substrand	Beginning ELD level *(Continued)*			
	Grades K–2	Grades 3–5	Grades 6–8	Grades 9–12
Comprehension and Analysis of Grade-Level-Appropriate Text		Identify, using key words and/or phrases, the main idea in a story read aloud.	Orally identify, using key words or phrases, the main ideas and some details of familiar texts.	Orally identify the main ideas and some details of familiar literature and informational materials/public documents (e.g., newspaper, brochure) by using key words or phrases.
		Point out text features, such as the title, table of contents, and chapter headings.	Point out text features, such as the title, table of contents, and chapter headings.	Point out text features, such as the title, table of contents, and chapter headings.
Structural Features of Informational Materials			Use pictures, lists, charts, and tables found in informational materials, newspapers, and magazines to identify the factual components of compare-and-contrast patterns.	Identify the vocabulary, syntax, and grammar used in public and workplace documents (e.g., speeches, debates, manuals, and contracts).
Comprehension and Analysis of Grade-Level-Appropriate Text and Expository Critique			Orally identify examples of fact and opinion and cause and effect in simple texts.	

Reading

Reading Comprehension

English–language arts substrand	Early intermediate ELD level			
	Grades K–2	Grades 3–5	Grades 6–8	Grades 9–12
Comprehension	Respond orally to simple stories read aloud, using phrases or simple sentences to answer factual comprehension questions.	Read and listen to simple stories and demonstrate understanding by using simple sentences to respond to explicit detailed questions (e.g., "The bear is brown").	Read and orally respond to simple literary texts and texts in content areas by using simple sentences to answer factual comprehension questions.	Read and orally respond to simple literary texts and texts in content areas by using simple sentences to answer factual comprehension questions.
	Draw and label pictures related to a story topic or one's own experience.	Read and orally identify relationships between written text and one's own experience by using simple sentences.		
	Understand and follow simple two-step directions for classroom activities.	Understand and follow simple two-step directions for classroom activities.	Identify and follow some multiple-step directions for using simple mechanical devices and filling out basic forms.	Identify and follow some multiple-step directions for using simple mechanical devices and filling out basic forms.
Comprehension and Analysis of Grade-Level-Appropriate Text	Orally identify, using key words or phrases, the basic sequence of events in text read aloud.	Orally identify, using simple sentences, the basic sequence of events in text that one reads.	Identify and orally explain categories of familiar informational materials by using simple sentences.	Orally identify the features of simple excerpts of public documents by using key words or phrases.
	Draw logical inferences from a story read aloud.	Read text and orally identify the main ideas by using simple sentences and drawing inferences about the text.	Read text and orally identify the main ideas and details of informational materials, literary text, and text in content areas by using simple sentences.	Read and orally identify a few specific facts in simple expository text, such as consumer and workplace documents and content area text.
		Read and identify basic text features such as the title, table of contents, and chapter headings.		

(Continued on p. 52)

Reading

Reading Comprehension

English–language arts substrand	Early intermediate ELD level *(Continued)*			
	Grades K–2	Grades 3–5	Grades 6–8	Grades 9–12
Comprehension and Analysis of Grade-Level-Appropriate Text and Expository Critique		Orally identify examples of fact and opinion in familiar texts read aloud.	Read and orally identify examples of fact and opinion and cause and effect in written texts by using simple sentences.	
Structural Features of Informational Materials			Orally identify the factual components of simple informational materials by using key words or phrases.	In simple sentences orally identify the structure and format of workplace documents (e.g., format, graphics, and headers).
				Read a consumer or workplace document in a group activity and present a brief oral report, demonstrating three or four simple steps necessary to achieve a specific goal or obtain a product.

Reading

Reading Comprehension

English–language arts substrand	Intermediate ELD level			
	Grades K–2	Grades 3–5	Grades 6–8	Grades 9–12
Comprehension and Analysis of Grade-Level-Appropriate Text	Read stories and respond orally in simple sentences to factual comprehension questions about the stories.	Use detailed sentences to respond orally to comprehension questions about text (e.g., "The brown bear lives with his family in the forest").	Read literature and respond orally to it by answering in detailed sentences factual comprehension questions.	In detailed sentences identify orally two to three examples of how clarity of text is affected by the repetition of important ideas and by syntax.
	While reading aloud in a group, point out basic text features, such as the title, table of contents, and chapter headings.	Read text and identify features, such as the title, table of contents, chapter headings, diagrams, charts, glossaries, and indexes in written texts.		Present a brief report that verifies and clarifies facts in two to three forms of expository text.
	Draw inferences about stories read aloud and use simple phrases or sentences to communicate the inferences.	Read text and use detailed sentences to identify orally the main ideas and use them to make predictions and support them with details.	Read text and use detailed sentences to explain orally the main ideas and details of informational text, literary text, and text in content areas.	Read text and use detailed sentences to identify orally the main ideas and use them to make predictions about informational text, literary text, and text in content areas.
Comprehension	Write captions or phrases for drawings related to a story.	Read and use more detailed sentences to describe orally the relationships between text and one's own experiences.		
	Understand and follow some multiple-step directions for classroom-related activities.	Understand and follow some multiple-step directions for classroom-related activities.	Understand and orally explain most multiple-step directions for using a simple mechanical device and filling out simple applications.	Understand and orally explain most multiple-step directions for using a simple mechanical device and filling out simple applications.

(Continued on p. 54)

Reading

Reading Comprehension

English–language arts substrand	Intermediate ELD level *(Continued)*			
	Grades K–2	Grades 3–5	Grades 6–8	Grades 9–12
Comprehension and Analysis of Grade-Level-Appropriate Text and Expository Critique		Read literature and content area texts and orally identify examples of fact and opinion and cause and effect.		
				Listen to an excerpt from a brief political speech and give an oral critique of the author's evidence by using simple sentences.
Structural Features of Informational Materials			Identify and use detailed sentences to explain orally the differences among some categories of informational materials.	Read workplace documents and orally identify the structure and format (e.g., graphics and headers) and give one brief example of how the author uses the feature to achieve his or her purpose.
			Understand and orally identify the features and elements of common consumer (e.g., warranties, contracts, manuals) and informational materials (e.g., magazines and books).	Read and use simple sentences to identify orally the features and the rhetorical devices of simple excerpts of public and workplace documents and content area texts.

Reading

Reading Comprehension

English–language arts substrand	Early advanced ELD level			
	Grades K–2	Grades 3–5	Grades 6–8	Grades 9–12
Comprehension and Analysis of Grade-Level-Appropriate Text	Read text and use detailed sentences to identify orally the main idea and use the idea to draw inferences about the text.	Describe the main ideas and supporting details of a text.	Identify and explain the main ideas and critical details of informational materials, literary texts, and texts in content areas.	Apply knowledge of language to achieve comprehension of informational materials, literary texts, and texts in content areas.
	Read stories and orally respond to them by answering factual comprehension questions about cause-and-effect relationships.	Generate and respond to comprehension questions related to the text.		
	Write a brief summary (three or four complete sentences) of a story.	Describe relationships between the text and one's personal experience.		
Comprehension	Read and use basic text features, such as the title, table of contents, and chapter headings.	Locate text features, such as format, diagrams, charts, glossaries, and indexes, and identify the functions.		
Comprehension and Analysis of Grade-Level-Appropriate Text and Expository Critique	Read stories and texts from content areas and respond orally to them by restating facts and details to clarify ideas.	Use the text (such as the ideas presented, illustrations, titles) to draw conclusions and make inferences.		Analyze the structure and format of work-place documents and the way in which authors use structure and format to achieve their purposes.
		Distinguish explicit examples of facts, opinions, inference, and cause and effect in texts.		Prepare oral and written reports that evaluate the credibility of an author's argument or defense of a claim (include a bibliography).

(Continued on p. 56)

Reading

Reading Comprehension

English–language arts substrand	Early advanced ELD level *(Continued)*			
	Grades K–2	Grades 3–5	Grades 6–8	Grades 9–12
Structural Features of Informational Materials		Identify some significant structural (organizational) patterns in text, such as sequential or chronological order and cause and effect.	Identify and explain the differences between various categories of informational materials (e.g., textbooks, newspapers, instructional materials).	Read material and analyze how clarity is affected by patterns of organization, repetition of key ideas, syntax, and word choice.
			Analyze a variety of rhetorical styles found in consumer (e.g., warranties, contracts, manuals) and informational materials (e.g., newspapers, magazines, and textbooks).	Analyze the features and rhetorical devices of at least two types of documents intended for the general public (e.g., warranties, contracts, manuals, magazines, and textbooks).

Reading

Reading Comprehension

English–language arts substrand	Advanced ELD level			
	Grades K–2	Grades 3–5	Grades 6–8	Grades 9–12
Comprehension and Analysis of Grade-Level-Appropriate Text	Prepare an oral or a written summary by using various comprehension strategies (e.g., generate and respond to questions, draw inferences, compare information from several sources) with literature and content area texts.	Use the text (such as the ideas, illustrations, titles) to draw inferences and conclusions and make generalizations.	Identify and explain the main ideas and critical details of informational materials, literary text, and text in content areas.	Apply knowledge of language to achieve comprehension of informational materials, literary text, and text in content areas.
Comprehension and Analysis of Grade-Level-Appropriate Text and Expository Critique		Describe main ideas and supporting details, including supporting evidence.		
	Locate and use text features, such as the title, table of contents, chapter headings, diagrams, and index.	Use text features, such as format, diagrams, charts, glossaries, indexes, and the like, to locate and draw information from text.	Analyze a variety of rhetorical styles, found in consumer (e.g., warranties, contracts) and informational materials (e.g., newspapers, magazines, signs, textbooks).	Analyze the features and rhetorical devices of different types of public documents and the way authors use those features and devices.
Structural Features of Informational Materials			Identify and analyze the differences between various categories of informational materials (textbooks, newspapers, instructional manuals, signs).	Analyze how clarity is affected by patterns of organization, hierarchical structures, repetition of key ideas, syntax, and word choice in texts across content areas.
		Identify significant structural (organizational) patterns in text, such as compare and contrast, sequential and chronological order, and cause and effect.		

(Continued on p. 58)

Reading

Reading Comprehension

English–language arts substrand	Advanced ELD level *(Continued)*			
	Grades K–2	Grades 3–5	Grades 6–8	Grades 9–12
Comprehension and Analysis of Grade-Level-Appropriate Text, Expository Critique, and Structural Features of Informational Materials				Prepare oral and written reports that evaluate the credibility of an author's argument or defense of a claim by critiquing the relationship between generalizations and evidence. Prepare a bibliography for the report.
				Prepare a brief research or synthesizing paper in a content area and analyze ideas from several sources to present a coherent argument or conclusion arranged in the proper format, including a bibliography.
		Distinguish fact from opinion and inference and cause from effect in text.		

Literary Response and Analysis

For English learners to improve their English skills and reduce the likelihood that those skills will level off before the students reach fluency, they need to learn academic content along with language skills. Instruction in academic areas, such as literature, mathematics, geography, history, government, and science, not only familiarizes learners with the content of the discipline, but also, what is more important, teaches them how to use the language required to communicate in the discipline (Mohan 1986). English learners at all fluency levels are highly motivated by instruction in academic subjects. They immediately see the value of learning to use English to meet their every-day needs and to help them succeed in school as they learn how to communicate in an academic area (Snow, Met, and Genesee 1989). Students whose English is not quite fluent may be motivated to work harder to develop English fluency so that they can communicate successfully in an academic area that they think may be important in their future.

Learning the reading, writing, speaking, and listening skills necessary to achieve English fluency is critical for English learners. Achieving fluency requires learning the basic structure of English (Gass and Selinker 1994). Literature is a critical component for developing fluency in English. Through literature the students are exposed to a broader range of English grammatical constructions and usage than they will generally experience in listening and speaking. Reading and responding to literature are also vehicles through which all students, including English learners, develop rich vocabularies. Teachers will frequently give students writing assignments for which they use literature as a model to produce an independent piece of writing. As English learners study literature, the opportunities increase for them to understand various literary features and use them in their own writing. This development in turn will enable them to move toward demonstrating proficiency in all the English–language arts standards.

At the lower ELD proficiency levels, reading materials should be at students' *developmental* proficiency level. *Grade-level* reading materials should be used with students who work at the advanced level. Students working at the advanced level of the ELD standards should also demonstrate proficiency in "Literary Response and Analysis" skills of the English–language arts standards. To ensure that students develop proficiency in both the ELD and the language arts standards, teachers must work concurrently with the two standards documents and the *Reading/Language Arts Framework* (1999).

Reading

Literary Response and Analysis

English–language arts substrand	Beginning ELD level			
	Grades K–2	Grades 3–5	Grades 6–8	Grades 9–12
Narrative Analysis of Grade-Level-Appropriate Text (*The standards are also addressed in "Reading Comprehension."*)	Listen to a story and respond orally in one or two words to factual comprehension questions.	Listen to a story and respond orally in one or two words to factual comprehension questions.	Respond orally in one or two words to factual comprehension questions about simple literary texts.	Identify orally the beginning, middle, and end of a simple literary text.
	Draw pictures related to a work of literature identifying setting and characters.	Identify orally different characters and settings in simple literary texts by using words or phrases.	Identify orally different characters and settings in simple literary texts by using words or phrases	Read a simple selection and orally identify the speaker or narrator.
			Role-play a character from a familiar piece of literature by using words and phrases.	Role-play a character from a familiar piece of literature by using phrases or simple sentences.
		Distinguish between fiction and nonfiction by giving one- or two-word oral responses.	Create pictures, lists, charts, and tables to identify the sequence of events in simple literary texts.	Create pictures, lists, charts, and tables to identify the sequence of events in simple literary texts.
				Recognize the difference in points of view between first person and third person by using phrases or simple sentences.
Structural Features of Literature		Create pictures, lists, charts, and tables to identify the characteristics of fairy tales, folktales, myths, and legends.	Create pictures, lists, and charts to orally identify the characteristics of three different forms of literature: fiction, nonfiction, and poetry.	
Narrative Analysis of Grade-Level-Appropriate Text (*The standards are also addressed in "Reading Comprehension."*)			Recite simple poems.	Recite simple poems.

Reading

Literary Response and Analysis

English–language arts substrand	Early intermediate ELD level			
	Grades K–2	Grades 3–5	Grades 6–8	Grades 9–12
Narrative Analysis of Grade-Level-Appropriate Text *(The standards are also addressed in "Reading Comprehension.")*	Respond orally to factual comprehension questions about stories by answering in simple sentences.	Respond orally to factual comprehension questions about brief literary texts by answering in simple sentences.	Respond orally to factual comprehension questions about brief literary texts by answering in simple sentences.	Respond orally in simple sentences to factual comprehension questions about two forms of literature (brief excerpts from a comedy and tragedy).
		Read literary texts and orally identify the main events of the plot by using simple sentences.	Read literary texts and orally identify the main events of the plot by using simple sentences.	Read literary texts and orally identify the main events of the plot by using simple sentences.
			Read a selection and orally identify the speaker or narrator.	
			Identify the difference in points of view between first person and third person by using simple sentences.	
	Recite simple poems.	Recite simple poems.		
Narrative Analysis of Grade-Level-Appropriate Text	Identify orally the setting and characters by using simple sentences and vocabulary.	Describe orally in simple sentences the setting of a literary work.		Identify orally the theme, plot, setting, and characters of a literary selection by using simple sentences.

(Continued on p. 62)

Reading

Literary Response and Analysis

English–language arts substrand	Early intermediate ELD level (Continued)			
	Grades K–2	Grades 3–5	Grades 6–8	Grades 9–12
Structural Features of Literature		Distinguish orally between poetry, drama, and short stories by using simple sentences.	Distinguish orally the characteristics of different forms of fiction and poetry by using simple sentences.	Distinguish the characteristics of different forms of dramatic literature (e.g., comedy and tragedy) by using simple sentences, pictures, lists, charts, and tables.
Narrative Analysis of Grade-Level-Appropriate Text and Literary Criticism		Describe orally in simple sentences a character in a literary selection according to his or her actions.	Describe orally in simple sentences a character in a brief literary text by identifying the thoughts and actions of the character.	Describe briefly in simple sentences a character according to what he or she does in a familiar narration, dialogue, or drama.
				Use expanded vocabulary and some descriptive words in oral responses to familiar literature.

Reading

Literary Response and Analysis

English–language arts substrand	Intermediate ELD level			
	Grades K–2	Grades 3–5	Grades 6–8	Grades 9–12
Narrative Analysis of Grade-Level-Appropriate Text *(The standards are also addressed in "Word Analysis, Fluency, and Systematic Vocabulary Development.")*	Use expanded vocabulary and descriptive words in oral and written responses to simple texts.	Use expanded vocabulary and descriptive words in paraphrasing oral and written responses to texts.	Use expanded vocabulary and descriptive words in paraphrasing oral and written responses to texts.	Use expanded vocabulary and descriptive words in paraphrasing oral and written responses to texts.
Narrative Analysis of Grade-Level-Appropriate Text *(The standards are also addressed in "Reading Comprehension.")*	Read simple poetry and use simple sentences in answering factual comprehension questions.		Read text and use detailed sentences to respond orally to factual comprehension questions about three forms of brief prose (e.g., short story, novel, essay).	Read text and use detailed sentences to respond orally to factual comprehension questions about three forms of literature.
				Read literary texts and use detailed sentences to describe orally the sequence of events.
		Apply knowledge of language to derive meaning from literary texts and comprehend them.	Apply knowledge of language to analyze and derive meaning from literary texts and comprehend them.	Apply knowledge of language to analyze and derive meaning from literary texts and comprehend them.
Narrative Analysis of Grade-Level-Appropriate Text and Literary Criticism				Use detailed sentences to compare and contrast orally a similar theme or topic across three genres.
				Read a literary selection and use detailed sentences to explain orally the elements of theme, plot, setting, and characters.

(Continued on p. 64)

Reading

Literary Response and Analysis

English–language arts substrand	Intermediate ELD level *(Continued)*			
	Grades K–2	Grades 3–5	Grades 6–8	Grades 9–12
Narrative Analysis of Grade-Level-Appropriate Text and Literary Criticism				Read a literary selection and use detailed sentences to describe orally a character according to what he or she does in a narration, dialogue, or dramatic monologue.
Structural Features of Literature				Use detailed sentences to orally identify at least two ways in which poets use personification, figures of speech, and sound.

Reading

Literary Response and Analysis

English–language arts substrand	Early advanced ELD level			
	Grades K–2	Grades 3–5	Grades 6–8	Grades 9–12
Structural Features of Literature	Read short poems and orally identify the basic elements (e.g., rhythm and rhyme)	Identify and describe figurative language (e.g., similes, metaphors, and personification)	Identify literary devices, such as narrative voice, symbolism, dialect, and irony	Identify several literary elements and techniques (e.g., figurative language, imagery, and symbolism).
		Distinguish between literary connotations and symbols from culture to culture.		Read and identify ways in which poets use personification, figures of speech, imagery, and the "sound" of language.
				Identify the functions of dialogue, scene design, and asides in dramatic literature.
		Read a literary selection and orally identify metaphors and similes.	Describe orally the major characteristics of several forms of poetry by using detailed sentences.	
Narrative Analysis of Grade-Level-Appropriate Text and Literary Criticism	Read a literary selection and orally identify the literary elements of plot, setting, and characters.	Identify the motives of characters in a work of fiction.	Describe the author's point of view in literary text by using detailed sentences.	
	Read a story and identify the beginning, middle, and end.	Recognize and describe themes stated directly in a text.	Compare and contrast a similar theme across several genres by using detailed sentences.	Compare and contrast orally and in writing a similar theme or topic across several genres by using detailed sentences.
		Read a literary selection and orally identify the speaker or narrator by using simple sentences.	Describe orally and in writing a similar theme or topic by using detailed sentences.	Identify recognized works of American literature and the genre to which they belong to contrast major periods, themes, and trends.

(Continued on p. 66)

Reading

Literary Response and Analysis

English–language arts substrand	Early advanced ELD level (Continued)			
	Grades K–2	Grades 3–5	Grades 6–8	Grades 9–12
Narrative Analysis of Grade-Level-Appropriate Text and Literary Criticism		Read a literary selection and orally identify the main conflict in the plot and its resolution.	Read a literary selection and orally explain the literary elements of plot, setting, and characters by using detailed sentences.	Identify recognized works of world literature and contrast the major literary forms and techniques.
			Describe the major characteristics of several forms of fiction and poetry: short story, essay, novel, ballad, lyric, epic.	Identify the characteristics of subgenres (e.g., satire, pastoral, allegory) that are used in various genres.
Narrative Analysis of Grade-Level-Appropriate Text		Recognize the difference between the first-person and third-person points of view in a literary text.		
Structural Features of Literature, Narrative Analysis of Grade-Level-Appropriate Text, and Literary Criticism				Identify techniques that have specific rhetorical or aesthetic purposes in literary texts (e.g., irony, tone, mood, "sound" of language).

Reading

Literary Response and Analysis

English–language arts substrand	Advanced ELD level			
	Grades K–2	Grades 3–5	Grades 6–8	Grades 9–12
Narrative Analysis of Grade-Level-Appropriate Text *(The standards are also addressed in "Reading Comprehension.")*	Read a variety of children's literature and respond to it both orally and in writing.			
Structural Features of Literature	Describe the elements of poetry (e.g., rhythm, rhyme, alliteration).	Describe the major characteristics of poetry, drama, fiction, and nonfiction.	Analyze the setting (place, time, customs) and its influence on the meaning of and conflict in a literary text.	Describe the functions of dialogue, scene design, asides, and soliloquies in drama.
Narrative Analysis of Grade-Level-Appropriate Text and Literary Criticism	Compare and contrast different authors' use of literary elements.	Identify various techniques to influence readers' perspectives and evaluate the author's use of the techniques.	Identify and describe several literary elements and techniques in literary texts (e.g., figurative language, imagery, and symbolism).	Explain the significance of several literary elements and techniques (e.g., figurative language, imagery, allegory, and symbolism).
		Recognize and describe themes stated directly or implied in literary texts.	Compare and contrast a similar theme or topic across genres and explain how the genre shapes the themes or topics.	Compare and contrast a similar theme or topic across genres and explain how the genre shapes the theme or topic.
			Analyze recurring themes across literary works (e.g., good and evil, loyalty and betrayal).	
		Compare and contrast the motives of characters in a work of fiction.	Compare and contrast the motivation and reactions of characters across a variety of literary texts.	Analyze the interaction between characters and subordinate characters in literary texts (e.g., motivations and reactions).

(Continued on p. 68)

Reading

Literary Response and Analysis

English–language arts substrand	Advanced ELD level *(Continued)*			
	Grades K–2	Grades 3–5	Grades 6–8	Grades 9–12
Narrative Analysis of Grade-Level-Appropriate Text and Literary Criticism			Analyze the elements of a plot, including its development and the way conflicts are addressed and resolved.	
				Analyze recognized works of American literature and identify their genre to contrast major periods and trends.
				Relate the literary works of authors to the major themes and issues of their eras.

Strategies and Applications

As English learners begin to develop language skills in listening, speaking, and reading, they also need to develop writing skills. Linguistic studies note that English learners will transfer language skills from their primary language to English (Odlin 1989), especially if similarities between English and the primary language exist and if students are substantially literate in their primary language. Research also indicates that integrating the four language skills (reading, writing, speaking, and listening) is crucial for English learners to develop the ability to write effectively (Mangeldorf 1989).

Reading is particularly important because it provides English learners with opportunities to acquire grammar, expand vocabulary, gain increasing fluency with written texts, and improve speaking skills (*Interactive Approaches to Second Language Reading* 1988). Reading provides students with model sentence patterns and linguistic structures. However, improved writing does not necessarily follow from reading. For English learners to apply their knowledge of sentence patterns and linguistic structures, they must put into practice what they observe from reading by engaging in various types of writing. If these students are to become successful users of English, their integrated instructional program must include numerous opportunities to develop writing skills.

Because English learners working at the advanced level of the ELD standards are also expected to demonstrate proficiency in the language arts standards, it is essential for teachers to use the two standards documents concurrently and to monitor students' progress on both sets of standards.

Writing

Strategies and Applications

English–language arts substrand	Beginning ELD level			
	Grades K–2	Grades 3–5	Grades 6–8	Grades 9–12
Penmanship	Copy the English alphabet legibly.	Write the English alphabet legibly.		
Penmanship and Organization and Focus	Copy words posted and commonly used in the classroom (e.g., labels, number names, days of the week).	Label key parts of common objects.	Organize and record information from selected literature and content areas by displaying it on pictures, lists, charts, and tables.	Organize and record information from selected literature and content areas by displaying it on pictures, lists, charts, and tables.
Organization and Focus	Write a few words or phrases about an event or character from a story read by the teacher.	Create simple sentences or phrases with some assistance.	Create simple sentences or phrases with some assistance.	Create simple sentences or phrases with some assistance.
	Write a phrase or simple sentence about an experience generated from a group story.	Use models to write short narratives.	Write a brief narrative by using a few simple sentences that include the setting and some details.	Write a brief narrative by using a few simple sentences that include the setting and some details.
		During group writing activities, write brief narratives and stories by using a few standard grammatical forms.	Use the writing process to write brief narratives and stories with a few standard grammatical forms.	Use the writing process to write brief narratives with a few standard grammatical forms.
			Write simple compositions, such as descriptions and comparison and contrast, that have a main idea and some detail.	Write simple compositions, such as descriptions and comparison and contrast, that have a main idea and some detail.
			Complete basic business forms in which information such as one's name, address, and telephone number is requested.	Complete a job application form by providing basic information, such as one's name, age, address, and education.

Writing

Strategies and Applications

English–language arts substrand	Early intermediate ELD level			
	Grades K–2	Grades 3–5	Grades 6–8	Grades 9–12
Organization and Focus	Write simple sentences about events or characters from familiar stories read aloud by the teacher.	Write short narrative stories that include elements of setting and characters.	Write simple sentences of brief responses to selected literature to show factual under standing of the text.	Write simple sentences to respond to selected literature, exhibit factual understanding of the text, and connect one's own experience to specific parts of the text.
	Write simple sentences by using key words posted and commonly used in the classroom (e.g., labels, number names, days of the week, and months (e.g., "Today is Tuesday").	Write simple sentences and use drawings, pictures, lists, charts, and tables to respond to familiar literature.	Use common verbs, nouns, and high-frequency modifiers in writing simple sentences.	Use common verbs, nouns, and high-frequency modifiers in writing simple sentences.
		Follow a model given by the teacher to independently write a short paragraph of at least four sentences.	Create a draft of a paragraph by following an outline.	Use simple sentences to create a draft of a short essay that follows an outline.
		Write an increasing number of words and simple sentences appropriate for language arts and other content areas (e.g., math, science, history–social science).	Write an increasing number of words and simple sentences appropriate for language arts and other content areas (e.g., math, science, history–social science).	Write an increasing number of words and simple sentences appropriate for language arts and other content areas (e.g., math, science, history–social science).
		Follow a model to write a friendly letter.	Write expository compositions, such as descriptions, compari-son and contrast, and problem and solution, that include a main idea and some details in simple sentences.	Write expository compositions, such as descriptions, compari-son and contrast, and problem and solution, that include a main idea and some details in simple sentences.

(Continued on p. 72)

Writing

Strategies and Applications

English–language arts substrand	Early intermediate ELD level *(Continued)*			
	Grades K–2	Grades 3–5	Grades 6–8	Grades 9–12
Organization and Focus			Collect information from various sources (e.g., dictionary, library books, research materials) and take notes on a given topic.	Collect information from various sources (e.g., dictionary, library books, research materials) and take notes on a given topic.
Organization and Focus, Evaluation and Revision	Write one to two simple sentences (e.g., "I went to the park").	Produce independent writing that is understood when read but may include inconsistent use of standard grammatical forms.	Proceed through the writing process to write short paragraphs that contain supporting details about a given topic. There may be some inconsistent use of standard grammatical forms.	Proceed through the writing process to write short paragraphs that contain supporting details about a given topic. There may be some inconsistent use of standard grammatical forms.
Organization and Focus, Research and Technology			Complete simple informational documents related to career development (e.g., bank forms and job applications).	Complete simple informational documents related to career development (e.g., bank forms and job applications).

Writing

Strategies and Applications

English–language arts substrand	Intermediate ELD level			
	Grades K–2	Grades 3–5	Grades 6–8	Grades 9–12
Organization and Focus	Write short narrative stories that include the elements of setting and characters.	Narrate with some detail a sequence of events.	Narrate a sequence of events and communicate their significance to the audience.	Narrate a sequence of events and communicate their significance to the audience.
	Produce independent writing that is understood when read but may include inconsistent use of standard grammatical forms.	Produce independent writing that is understood when read but may include inconsistent use of standard grammatical forms.	Write brief expository compositions (e.g., description, comparison and contrast, cause and effect, and problem and solution) that include a thesis and some points of support.	Write brief expository compositions and reports that (a) include a thesis and some supporting details; (b) provide information from primary sources; and (c) include charts and graphs.
	Following a model, proceed through the writing process to independently write short paragraphs of at least three lines.	Begin to use a variety of genres in writing (e.g., expository, narrative, poetry).	Develop a clear purpose in a short essay by appropriately using the rhetorical devices of quotations and facts.	Recognize elements of characterization in a piece of writing and apply the same techniques when writing.
		Independently create cohesive paragraphs that develop a central idea with consistent use of standard English grammatical forms. (Some rules may not be followed.)	Write responses to selected literature that exhibit understanding of the text, using detailed sentences and transitions.	Write responses to selected literature that exhibit understanding of the text, using detailed sentences and transitions.
	Write simple sentences appropriate for language arts and other content areas (e.g., math, science, social studies).	Use more complex vocabulary and sentences appropriate for language arts and other content areas (e.g., math, science, history–social science).	Use more complex vocabulary and sentences appropriate for language arts and other content areas (e.g., math, science, history–social science).	Recognize structured ideas and arguments and support examples in persuasive writing.

(Continued on p. 74)

Writing

Strategies and Applications

English–language arts substrand	Intermediate ELD level *(Continued)*			
	Grades K–2	Grades 3–5	Grades 6–8	Grades 9–12
Organization and Focus	Write a friendly letter of a few lines.	Write a letter independently by using detailed sentences.	Write documents related to career development (e.g., business letter, job application).	Fill out job applications and prepare résumés that are clear and provide all needed information.
			Use complex sentences in writing brief fictional biographies and short stories that include a sequence of events and supporting details.	Use complex sentences in writing brief fictional biographies and short stories that include a sequence of events and supporting details.
Organization and Focus, Research and Technology			Use basic strategies of notetaking, outlining, and the writing process to structure drafts of simple essays, with consistent use of standard grammatical forms. (Some rules may not be followed.)	Use basic strategies of notetaking, outlining, and the writing process to structure drafts of simple essays, with consistent use of standard grammatical forms. (Some rules may not be followed.)
			Investigate and research a topic in a content area and develop a brief essay or report that includes source citations.	Investigate and research a topic in a content area and develop a brief essay or report that includes source citations.

Writing

Strategies and Applications

English–language arts substrand	Early advanced ELD level			
	Grades K–2	Grades 3–5	Grades 6–8	Grades 9–12
Organization and Focus	Write short narratives that include elements of setting, characters, and events.	Write a detailed summary of a story.	Write in different genres (e.g., short stories and narratives), including coherent plot development, characterization, and setting.	Identify in writing the various elements of discourse (e.g., purpose, speaker, audience, form).
	Proceed through the writing process to write short paragraphs that maintain a consistent focus.	Arrange compositions according to simple organizational patterns.	Develop a clear thesis and support it by using analogies, quotations, and facts appropriately.	Develop a clear thesis and support it by using analogies, quotations, and facts appropriately.
		Independently write simple responses to literature.	Write responses to selected literature that develop interpretations, exhibit careful reading, and cite specific parts of the text.	Write persuasive compositions that structure ideas and arguments in a logical way with consistent use of standard grammatical forms.
	Use complex vocabulary and sentences appropriate for language arts and other content areas (e.g., math, science, social studies).	Use complex vocabulary and sentences appropriate for language arts and other content areas (e.g., math, science, social studies).	Use appropriate language variations and genres in writing for language arts and other content areas.	Use appropriate language variations and genres in writing for language arts and other content areas.
	Write a formal letter.	Independently write a persuasive letter with relevant evidence.	Write pieces related to career development (e.g., business letter, job application, letter of inquiry).	Fill out job applications and prepare résumés that are clear and purposeful and address the intended audience appropriately.

(Continued on p. 76)

Writing

Strategies and Applications

English–language arts substrand	Early advanced ELD level *(Continued)*			
	Grades K–2	Grades 3–5	Grades 6–8	Grades 9–12
Organization and Focus, Evaluation and Revision	Produce independent writing with consistent use of standard grammatical forms. (Some rules may not be followed.)	Write multiple-paragraph narrative and expository compositions appropriate for content areas, with consistent use of standard grammatical forms.	Write persuasive and expository compositions that include a clear thesis, describe organized points of support, and address a counterargument.	Write reflective compositions that explore the significance of events.
			Write detailed fictional biographies or autobiographies.	Write detailed fictional biographies or autobiographies.
Organization and Focus, Research and Technology, Evaluation and Revision			Use strategies of notetaking, outlining, and summarizing to structure drafts of clear, coherent, and focused essays with consistent use of standard grammatical forms.	Use strategies of notetaking, outlining, and summarizing to structure drafts of clear, coherent, and focused essays with consistent use of standard grammatical forms.
Organization and Focus, Research and Technology			Write an essay or report that balances information, has original ideas, and gives credit to sources in a bibliography. Use appropriate tone and voice for the purpose, audience, and subject matter.	Write expository compositions and reports that convey information from primary and secondary sources and use some technical terms. Use appropriate tone and voice for the purpose, audience, and subject matter.

Writing

Strategies and Applications

English–language arts substrand	Advanced ELD level			
	Grades K–2	Grades 3–5	Grades 6–8	Grades 9–12
Organization and Focus	Write short narratives that include examples of writing appropriate for language arts and other content areas (e.g., math, science, social studies).	Write short narratives that include examples of writing appropriate for language arts and other content areas (e.g., math, science, social studies).	Write persuasive expository compositions that include a clear thesis, describe organized points of support, and address counterarguments.	Write persuasive and expository compositions that include a clear thesis, describe organized points of support, and address counterarguments.
		Write a persuasive composition by using standard grammatical forms.	Produce writing by using various elements of discourse (e.g., purpose, speaker, audience, form) in narrative, expository, persuasive, and/or descriptive writing.	Produce writing that establishes a controlling impression or thesis.
	Write short narratives that describe the setting, characters, objects, and events.	Write narratives that describe the setting, characters, objects, and events.	Use appropriate language variations and genres in writing for language arts and other content areas.	Structure ideas and arguments in a given context by giving supporting and relevant examples.
			Write pieces related to career development (e.g., business letter, job application, letter of inquiry, memorandum).	Complete job applications and write résumés that fit the purpose and audience and follow the conventional format for the type of document.
Organization and Focus, Evaluation and Revision	Produce independent writing by using correct grammatical forms.	Write multiple-paragraph narrative and expository compositions by using standard grammatical forms.	Write responses to literature that develop interpretations, exhibit careful reading, and cite specific parts of the text.	Produce writing by using various elements of discourse (e.g., purpose, speaker, audience, form) in narrative, expository, persuasive, and/or descriptive writing.

(Continued on p. 78)

Writing

Strategies and Applications

English–language arts substrand	Advanced ELD level *(Continued)*			
	Grades K–2	Grades 3–5	Grades 6–8	Grades 9–12
Organization and Focus, Evaluation and Revision	Proceed through the writing process to write clear and coherent sentences and paragraphs that maintain a consistent focus.	Independently use all the steps of the writing process.	Develop a clear thesis and use various rhetorical devices (e.g., analogies, quotations, facts, statistics, and comparison) to support it.	Use various rhetorical devices (e.g., appeal to logic through reasoning, case study, and analogy) to support assertions.
Organization and Focus, Research and Technology			Use strategies of notetaking, outlining, and summarizing to structure drafts of clear, coherent, and focused essays by using standard grammatical forms.	Use strategies of notetaking, outlining, and summarizing to structure drafts of clear, coherent, and focused essays by using standard grammatical forms.
			Write documents (e.g., fictional biographies, autobiographies, short stories, and narratives) that include coherent plot development, characterization, setting, and a variety of literary strategies (e.g., dialogue, suspense).	Write expository compositions, including analytical essays and research reports, for the language arts and other content areas and provide evidence in support of a thesis and related claims.
			Use various methods of investigation and research to develop an essay or report that balances information and original ideas, including a bibliography.	Clarify and defend positions with relevant evidence, including facts, expert opinions, quotations, and/or expressions of commonly accepted beliefs and logical reasoning.

WRITING

English-Language Conventions

The ELD standards identify the stages that English learners must pass through to use the conventions of English effectively in writing. Depending on the degree to which their primary language differs from English in its written form and the degree to which students are already proficient writers in their primary language, English learners face unique challenges as they work to successfully use the conventions of written English.

At all ELD proficiency levels, English learners are to produce writing that includes correct capitalization, punctuation, and spelling of words appropriate to the students' developing fluency in English. By the advanced level, the students are to demonstrate proficiency in both the ELD and the language arts standards for their current grade level and for all prior grade levels.

Writing

English-Language Conventions

English–language arts substrand	Beginning ELD level			
	Grades K–2	Grades 3–5	Grades 6–8	Grades 9–12
Capitalization	Use capitalization when writing one's own name.	Use capitalization when writing one's own name and at the beginning of sentences.		
Punctuation		Use a period at the end of a sentence and a question mark at the end of a question.	Edit one's own work and correct the punctuation.	Edit one's own work and correct the punctuation.
Sentence Structure, Grammar, Punctuation, Capitalization, and Spelling			Identify basic vocabulary, mechanics, and sentence structures in a piece of writing.	Identify basic vocabulary, mechanics, and sentence structures in a piece of writing.
			Revise one's writing for proper use of final punctuation, capitalization, and correct spelling.	Revise one's writing for proper use of final punctuation, capitalization, and correct spelling.

Writing

English-Language Conventions

English–language arts substrand	Early intermediate ELD level			
	Grades K–2	Grades 3–5	Grades 6–8	Grades 9–12
Capitalization	Use capitalization to begin sentences and for proper nouns.	Use capitalization to begin sentences and for proper nouns.		
Punctuation	Use a period or question mark at the end of a sentence.	Use a period at the end of a sentence and use some commas appropriately.		
Punctuation, Capitalization, and Spelling	Edit writing for basic conventions (e.g., capitalization and use of periods) and make some corrections.	Edit writing for basic conventions (e.g., punctuation, capitalization, and spelling) and make some corrections.	Edit writing for basic conventions (e.g., punctuation, capitalization, and spelling).	Edit writing for basic conventions (e.g., punctuation, capitalization, and spelling).
Sentence Structure, Grammar, Punctuation, and Capitalization			Revise writing, with teacher's assistance, to clarify meaning and improve the mechanics and organization.	Revise writing, with teacher's assistance, to clarify meaning and improve the mechanics and organization.
			Use clauses, phrases, and mechanics of writing with consistent variations in grammatical forms.	Use clauses, phrases, and mechanics of writing with consistent variations in grammatical forms.

Writing

English-Language Conventions

English–language arts substrand	Intermediate ELD level			
	Grades K–2	Grades 3–5	Grades 6–8	Grades 9–12
Capitalization, Punctuation, and Spelling	Produce independent writing that may include some inconsistent use of capitalization, periods, and correct spelling.	Produce independent writing that may include some inconsistent use of capitalization, periods, and correct spelling.		
Sentence Structure, Grammar, and Spelling	Use standard word order but may have some inconsistent grammatical forms (e.g., subject/verb without inflections).	Use standard word order but may have inconsistent grammatical forms (e.g., subject/verb agreement).	Revise writing for appropriate word choice and organization with variation in grammatical forms and spelling.	Revise writing for appropriate word choice and organization with variation in grammatical forms and spelling.
Sentence Structure, Grammar, Punctuation, Capitalization, and Spelling			Edit and correct basic grammatical structures and usage of the conventions of writing.	Edit and correct basic grammatical structures and usage of the conventions of writing.

Writing

English-Language Conventions

English–language arts substrand	Early advanced ELD level			
	Grades K–2	Grades 3–5	Grades 6–8	Grades 9–12
Capitalization, Punctuation, and Spelling	Produce independent writing that may include some periods, correct spelling, and inconsistent capitalization.	Produce independent writing with consistent use of correct capitalization, punctuation, and spelling	Create coherent paragraphs through effective transitions.	Create coherent paragraphs through effective transitions.
Sentence Structure, Grammar, and Spelling	Use standard word order with some inconsistent grammar forms (e.g., subject/verb agreement).	Use standard word order but may have more consistent grammatical forms, including inflections.	Revise writing for appropriate word choice, organization, consistent point of view, and transitions, with some variation in grammatical forms and spelling.	Revise writing for appropriate word choice, organization, consistent point of view, and transitions, with some variation in grammatical forms and spelling.
Punctuation, Capitalization, and Spelling	Edit writing to check some of the mechanics of writing (e.g., capitalization and periods).	Edit writing to check the basic mechanics of writing (e.g., punctuation, capitalization, and spelling).	Edit writing for grammatical structures and the mechanics of writing.	Edit writing for grammatical structures and the mechanics of writing.
	English–Language Arts Content Standards **Grade One: Spelling** 1.8 Spell three- and four-letter short-vowel words and grade-level-appropriate sight words correctly. **Grade Two** 1.7 Spell frequently used, irregular words correctly (e.g., *was, were, says, said, who, what, why*).	***English–Language Arts Content Standards*** **Grade Three: Spelling** 1.8 Spell correctly one-syllable words that have blends, contractions, compounds, orthographic patterns (e.g., *qu*, consonant doubling, changing the ending of a word from *–y* to *–ies* when forming the plural), and common homophones (e.g., *hair-hare*). 1.9 Arrange words in alphabetic order. **Grade Four** 1.7 Spell correctly roots, inflections, suffixes and prefixes, and syllable constructions.		

Writing

English-Language Conventions

English–language arts substrand	Advanced ELD level			
	Grades K–2	Grades 3–5	Grades 6–8	Grades 9–12
Sentence Structure and Grammar	Use complete sentences and correct word order.	Use complete sentences and correct word order.	Revise writing for appropriate word choice and organization, consistent point of view, and transitions, using approximately standard grammatical forms and spelling.	Revise writing for appropriate word choice and organization, consistent point of view, and transitions, using approximately standard grammatical forms and spelling.
Grammar	Use correct parts of speech, including correct subject/verb agreement.	Use correct parts of speech, including correct subject/verb agreement.	Create coherent paragraphs through effective transitions and parallel constructions.	Create coherent paragraphs through effective transitions and parallel constructions.
Capitalization, Punctuation, and Spelling	Edit writing for punctuation, capitalization, and spelling.	Edit writing for punctuation, capitalization, and spelling.	Edit writing for the mechanics to approximate standard grammatical forms.	Edit writing for the mechanics to approximate standard grammatical forms.
Sentence Structure, Grammar, Punctuation, Capitalization, and Spelling	Produce writing that demonstrates a command of the conventions of standard English.	Produce writing that demonstrates a command of the conventions of standard English.		

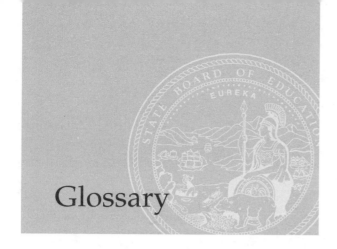

Glossary

affix
A word part that changes the meaning or function of a root or stem word to which it is attached.

alliteration
The occurrence in a phrase, line of speech, or writing of two or more words with the same initial sound.

cognates
Words in different languages related to the same root (e.g., *education* in English, *educación* in Spanish).

false cognates
Words from different languages that sound alike and are similar in form but are unrelated in meaning (e.g., *éxito* in Spanish means "success").

independent reading
The student reads text independently without the assistance of the teacher or other adult/tutor. The student also makes reading selections independently (e.g., from the classroom shelf, school library, or public library).

morphemes
Refers to the smallest unit of meaningful sound in language (i.e., words or affixes). There are two classes of morphemes: bound and free. Bound morphemes are meaning units that can never be a word by themselves (e.g., prefixes such as *re* in *redo* or suffixes such as *ment* in *establishment*). Free morphemes are equivalent to words (e.g., table, school, pencil).

phonemes
Smallest units of sound in language that are used to contrast words and the morphemes that make up words. Each language has a unique set of sounds, and English learners must master these sounds to a certain level of proficiency to understand English or orally communicate in English. Generally, older children and adults do not achieve full mastery of the production of these sounds and consequently speak English with an accent.

phonics
A system of teaching initial reading and spelling that stresses basic sound–symbol relationships and their application in decoding words.

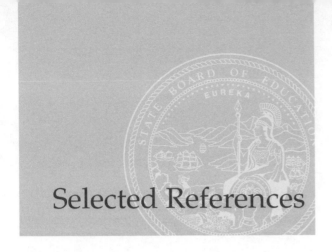

Selected References

Brinton, D. M.; M. A. Snow; and M. Wesche. 1989. *Content-based Second Language Instruction*. New York: Newbury House/Harper and Row.

Canale, M., and M. Swain. 1980. "Theoretical Bases of Communicative Approaches to Second Language Teaching and Testing," *Applied Linguistics*, Vol. 1, 1–47.

Collier, V. 1992. "A Synthesis of Studies Examining Long-term Language Minority Student Data in Academic Achievement," *Bilingual Research Journal*, Vol. 16, 187–212.

Crystal, D. 1987. *The Cambridge Encyclopedia of Language*. Cambridge, England: Cambridge University Press.

English–Language Arts Content Standards for California Public Schools, Kindergarten Through Grade Twelve. 1998. Sacramento: California Department of Education.

Ferris, D. 1994. "Rhetorical Strategies in Student Persuasive Writing: Differences Between Native and Non-native English Speakers," *Research in the Teaching of English*, Vol. 26, 45–65.

Gass, S. C., and L. Selinker. 1994. *Second Language Acquisition: An Introductory Course*. Hillsdale, N.J.: Lawrence Erlbaum Associates.

Halliday, M. A. K., and R. Hasan. 1976. *Cohesion in English*. London: Longman.

Hatch, E. 1983. *Psycholinguistics: A Second Language Perspective*. Rowley, Mass.: Newbury House.

Hughley, J. B., and others. 1983. *Teaching ESL Composition: Principles and Techniques*. Rowley, Mass.: Newbury House.

Ingram, D. 1989. *First Language Acquisition: Method, Description, and Explanation*. Cambridge, England: Cambridge University Press.

Interactive Approaches to Second Language Reading. 1988. Edited by P. Carrell, J. Devine, and D. Eskey. Cambridge, England: Cambridge University Press.

Kemper, S. 1984. "The Development of Narrative Skills: Explanations and Entertainments," in *Discourse Development: Progress in Cognitive Development*. Edited by S. A. Kuczaj. New York: Springer-Verlag, pp. 99–122.

Laufer, B. 1997. "The Lexical Plight in Second Language Reading: Words You Don't Know, Words You Think You Know and Words You Can't Guess," in *Second Language Vocabulary Acquisition: A Rationale for Pedagogy*. Edited by J. Coady and T. Huckin. New York: Cambridge University Press, pp. 20–52.

Long, M. H. 1983. "Does Second Language Instruction Make a Difference? A Review of Research," *Teaching English as a Second Language Quarterly*, Vol. 14, 378–90.

Mangeldorf, K. 1989. "Parallels Between Speaking and Writing in Second Language Acquisition," in *Richness in Writing: Empowering Language Minority Students*. Edited by D. M. Johnson and D. H. Roen. New York: Longman, pp. 134–45.

McCarthy, M. 1991. *Discourse Analysis for Language Teachers*. Cambridge, England: Cambridge University Press.

Mohan, B. 1986. *Content-based Language Instruction*. Reading, Mass.: Addison-Wesley.

Moskowitz, A. 1973. "On the Status of Vowel Shift in English," in *Cognitive Development and the Acquisition of Language*. Edited by T. E. Moore. New York: Academic Press.

Odlin, T. 1989. *Language Transfer: Cross-Linguistic Influence in Language Learning*. Cambridge, England: Cambridge University Press.

Omaggio, A. 1986. *Teaching Language in Context: Proficiency-oriented Instruction*. Boston: Heinle & Heinle Publishers.

Reading/Language Arts Framework for California Public Schools, Kindergarten Through Grade Twelve. 1999. Sacramento: California Department of Education.

Renkema, J. 1993. *Discourse Studies: An Introductory Textbook*. Amsterdam: John Benjamins Publishing Co.

Richard-Amato, P. A. 1988. *Making It Happen: Interaction in the Second Language Classroom: From Theory to Practice*. New York: Longman.

Scarcella, R. 1983. "Developmental Trends in the Acquisition of Conversational Competence by Adult Second Language Learners," in *Sociolinguistics and Language Acquisition*. Edited by N. Wolfson and E. Judd. Rowley, Mass.: Newbury House, pp. 175–83.

Scarcella, R. C., and R. L. Oxford. 1992. *The Tapestry of Language Learning: The Individual in the Communicative Classroom*. Boston: Heinle and Heinle Publishers.

Selinker, L. 1972. "Interlanguage," *International Review of Applied Linguistics in Language Teaching*, Vol. 10, 209–30.

Selinker, L., and D. Douglas. 1989. "Research Methodology in Contextually-based Second Language Research," *Second Language Research*, Vol. 5, 1–34.

Snow, M. A.; M. Met; and F. Genesee. 1989. "A Conceptual Framework for the Integration of Language and Content in Second/Foreign Language Instruction," *Teaching English as a Second Language Quarterly*, Vol. 23, 201–17.

Tharpe, R. G., and R. Gallimore. 1988. *Rousing Minds to Life: Teaching, Learning, and Schooling in Social Context*. Cambridge, England: Cambridge University Press.

Publications Available from the Department of Education

This publication is one of over 700 that are available from the California Department of Education. Some of the more recent publications or those most widely used are the following:

Item no.	Title (Date of publication)	Price
001559	Aiming High: High Schools for the Twenty-first Century (2002)	$13.25
001372	Arts Work: A Call for Arts Education for All California Students: The Report of the Superintendent's Task Force on the Visual and Performing Arts (1997)	11.25
001379	Assessing and Fostering the Development of a First and a Second Language in Early Childhood—Training Manual (1998)	19.00
001377	Assessing the Development of a First and a Second Language in Early Childhood: Resource Guide (1998)	10.75
001584	Bullying at School (2003)	14.25
001583	California Public School Directory 2003	19.50
001557	California Special Education Programs: A Composite of Laws (Twenty-fourth Edition) (2002)	20.00
001439	Check It Out! Assessing School Library Media Programs: A Guide for School District Education Policy and Implementation Teams (1998)	9.25
001476	Educating English Learners for the Twenty-First Century: The Report of the Proposition 227 Task Force (1999)	10.50
001509	Elementary Makes the Grade! (2000)	10.25
001389	English–Language Arts Content Standards for California Public Schools, Kindergarten Through Grade Twelve (1998)	9.25
001475	First Class: A Guide for Early Primary Education, Preschool–Kindergarten–First Grade (1999)	15.00
001570	Foreign Language Framework for California Public Schools, Kindergarten Through Grade Twelve (2003)	15.50
001574	Health Framework for California Public Schools, Kindergarten Through Grade Twelve (2003)	17.50
001477	Helping Your Students with Homework (1999)	9.25
001488	History–Social Science Content Standards for California Public Schools, Kindergarten Through Grade Twelve (2000)	9.00
001531	History–Social Science Framework for California Public Schools, Kindergarten Through Grade Twelve, 2001 Updated Edition with Content Standards (2001)	13.50
001442	Joining Hands: Preparing Teachers to Make Meaningful Home-School Connections (1998)	13.25
001556	Learning . . . Teaching . . . Leading: Report of the Professional Development Task Force (2002)	13.50
001266	Literature for the Visual and Performing Arts, Kindergarten Through Grade Twelve (1996)	10.25
001457	Mathematics Content Standards for California Public Schools, Kindergarten Through Grade Twelve (1999)	8.50
001508	Mathematics Framework for California Public Schools, Kindergarten Through Grade Twelve (2000 Revised Edition)	17.50
001384	Observing Preschoolers: Assessing First and Second Language Development (video) (1998)	12.00
001065	Physical Education Framework for California Public Schools, Kindergarten Through Grade Twelve (1994)	7.75
001555	Positive Intervention for Serious Behavior Problems: Best Practices in Implementing the Hughes Bill (Assembly Bill 2586) and the Positive Behavioral Intervention Regulations (Updated Revised Edition) (2001)	14.00
001222	Practical Ideas for Teaching Writing as a Process at the High School and College Levels (1997)	18.00
001514	Prekindergarten Learning and Development Guidelines (2000)	13.50
001289	Program Guidelines for Students Who Are Visually Impaired, 1997 Revised Edition	10.00
001502	Programs for Deaf and Hard of Hearing Students: Guidelines for Quality Standards (2000)	12.00
001549	Putting It All Together: Program Guidelines and Resources for State-Mandated HIV/AIDS Prevention Education in California Middle and High Schools (2003)	35.00
001462	Reading/Language Arts Framework for California Public Schools, Kindergarten Through Grade Twelve (1999)	17.50
001533	Recommended Literature: Kindergarten Through Grade Twelve (2002)	38.00
001562	Safe Schools: A Planning Guide for Action, 2002 Edition	12.00
001561	Safe Schools: A Planning Guide for Action Workbook, 2002 Edition	9.50
001511	SB 65 School-Based Pupil Motivation and Maintenance Program Guidelines (2000-01 Edition)	10.00
001505	School Attendance Improvement Handbook (2000)	14.25
001496	Science Content Standards for California Public Schools, Kindergarten Through Grade Twelve (2000)	9.00
001572	Science Framework for California Public Schools, Kindergarten Through Grade Twelve (2003)	17.50
001573	School Attendance Review Boards Handbook (2002)	15.50
001452	Service-Learning: Linking Classrooms and Communities: The Report of the Superintendent's Service Learning Task Force (1999)	7.00
001532	Standards for Evaluating Instructional Materials for Social Content (2000 Edition) (2001)	8.00
001407	Steering by Results—A High-Stakes Rewards and Interventions Program for California Schools and Students: The Report of the Rewards and Interventions Advisory Committee (1998)	8.00
001472	Strategic Teaching and Learning: Standards-Based Instruction to Promote Content Literacy in Grades Four Through Twelve (2000)	15.00
001383	Talking with Preschoolers: Strategies for Promoting First and Second Language Development (video) (1998)	12.00
001503	Taking Center Stage: A Commitment to Standards-Based Education for California's Middle-Grades Students (2001)	13.50
001392	Work-Based Learning Guide (1998)	12.50
001575	Work Permit Handbook for California Schools: Laws and Regulations Governing the Employment of Minors (2003)	18.00

Prices and availability are subject to change without notice. Please call 1-800-995-4099 for current prices and shipping charges.

Order Form

BUSINESS HOURS: 8:00 A.M.–4:30 P.M., PST

To order call: 1-800-995-4099

MONDAY THROUGH FRIDAY • FAX 916-323-0823

FROM:

SCHOOL/DISTRICT (if applicable)   ☐ PUBLIC   ☐ PRIVATE

NAME/ATTENTION

ADDRESS

CITY   STATE   ZIP CODE

( )

COUNTY   DAYTIME TELEPHONE

E-MAIL ADDRESS

PAYMENT METHOD: ☐ CHECK (Payable to California Department of Education)
☐ VISA
☐ MASTERCARD
☐ PURCHASE ORDER

CREDIT CARD NUMBER

EXPIRATION DATE

AUTHORIZED SIGNATURE

Item No.	Title	Quantity	Price each	Total
001578	*English-Language Development Standards for California Public Schools*		$12.50	$

SUBTOTAL	$
California residents add sales tax.	$
Shipping and handling charges (See chart at left.)	$
TOTAL	$

SHIPPING AND HANDLING CHARGES

Purchase amount	Add
0 - $15	$ 5.95
$15.01 - $30	7.95
$30.01 - $50	9.95
$50.01 - $100	11.95
$100.01 - $150	13.95
$150.01 - $200	15.95
$200.01 - $250	17.95
$250.01 - $300	19.95
$300.01 - $350	21.95
$350.01 and up	6% of subtotal

Mail completed order form to:

**California Department of Education
CDE Press Sales Office
1430 N Street, Suite 3207
Sacramento, CA 95814-5901**

Or fax completed order form to: **916-323-0823**

Visit our Web site: **http://www.cde.ca.gov/cdepress**

☐ **Please send me a free copy of the current *Educational Resources Catalog*.**

Note: Mail orders must be accompanied by a check, a purchase order, or a VISA or MasterCard credit card number, including expiration date and your signature. Purchase orders without checks are accepted from educational institutions, businesses, and governmental agencies. Purchase orders and credit card orders may be placed by FAX (916) 323-0823. Telephone orders will be accepted toll-free (1-800-995-4099) for credit card purchases. Please do not send cash. Stated prices are subject to change. Please order carefully; include correct item number and quantity for each publication ordered. *All sales are final after 30 days.*

PRICES AND AVAILABILITY OF PUBLICATIONS ARE SUBJECT TO CHANGE WITHOUT NOTICE.

R04-015 503-0003-05 8/05 20M
UNION LABEL OSP 05 92137